IDAHO HISTORY

1800 to Present

Skip Myers   **Justin Smith**

MacIntyre Purcell Publishing Inc.
Lunenburg, Nova Scotia

MacIntyre Purcell Publishing Inc.
194 Hospital Rd.
Lunenburg, Nova Scotia
B0J 2C0
(902) 640-3350
www.macintyrepurcell.com
info@macintyrepurcell.com

Printed and bound in Canada by Friesens

Cover design: Gwen North
Book design: Gwen North

Cover photo: Steam locomotives, boats, and even tractors helped build Idaho during the Industrial era. Such machines transformed the drudgery of manual labor, the frustration of tired work animals, and the slow progress of traditional methods of work. Seemingly overnight, Idaho transformed from the Old West to an industrial mining and agricultural powerhouse. *Photo by Clarence Bisbee.*

ISBN: 978-1-77276-168-9

Library and Archives Canada Cataloguing in Publication

Title: Idaho history : 1800 to present / Skip Myers, Justin Smith.
Names: Myers, Skip, author. | Smith, Justin (Justin J.), author.
Identifiers: Canadiana 2022014091X | ISBN 9781772761689 (hardcover)
Subjects: LCSH: Idaho—History. | LCSH: Idaho—History—Pictorial works. | LCSH: Idaho—History—
    Anecdotes.
Classification: LCC F746 .M94 2022 | DDC 979.6—dc23

AN IDAHO TIMELINE

1805: Lewis and Clark enter Idaho at Lemhi Pass.

1809: Kullyspell House fur trading post built near Lake Pend d'Oreille.

1810: Fort Henry established near St. Anthony

1811: First fur traders, the Astorians, explore route through Idaho.

1812: Donald Mackenzie establishes fur trading post about four miles east of the present site of Lewiston.

1813: John Reid opens fur post on Boise River.

1818: Donald Mackenzie explores Southern Idaho region with Snake River Expedition.

1818: U.S. and Great Britain Joint Occupation Treaty for Oregon Territory (including Idaho region).

1819: Adams-Onis treaty establishes Idaho's southern border at 42nd parallel.

1823: Lemhi Valley Battle between Piegan Indians and Snake River country expedition.

1824: Alexander Ross and Jedediah Smith explorations.

1824: Peter Skene Ogden begins trapping in Idaho.

1831: Kit Carson and Rocky Mountain Fur Company trappers winter on the Salmon River.

1832: Battle of Pierre's Hole between fur trappers and Gros Ventre tribe.

1832: Captain Bonneville brings first covered wagons over Rockies and arrives on the Lemhi river, followed by Snake and Salmon River area exploration.

1834: Nathaniel Wyeth establishes Fort Hall.

1834: Thomas McKay erects Fort Boise for Hudson's Bay Company.

1836: Eliza Spalding is the first white woman to travel overland to the Northwest. Henry Spalding develops Idaho's first irrigation system at Lapwai and grows first potatoes in Idaho. He establishes mission and Idaho's first school.

1842: Father Point establishes Jesuit Coeur d'Alene Mission of the Sacred Heart, Saint Maries.

1843: First Oregon Trail wagons cross Idaho.

1846: Oregon boundary dispute resolved. between England and the U.S. placing the border at 49 degrees latitude.

1849: California gold rush begins; 20,000 emigrants pass through Idaho on California trail.

1852: Gold discovered on the Pend d'Oreille River.

1853: Washington Territory created (included Idaho).

1854: Ward Massacre in Boise Valley.

1855: Mormon Salmon River mission established, Fort Lemhi.

1858: Bannock Indians attack Fort Lemhi forcing Mormons to abandon the site.

1860: Franklin is established as the first town in Idaho.

1860-62: Gold discovered at Orofino Creek, Salmon River and Boise Basin.

1861: Lewiston established.

1861: U.S. Civil War begins, Idaho gold to become a key resource for the Union.

1862: Idaho's first newspaper, *The Golden Age,* is published in Lewiston.

1863: Bear River Massacre.

1863: Boise Barracks (later Fort Boise) established by U.S. Cavalry.

1863: Idaho becomes territory.

1863: Owyhee mines open.

1863: Soda Springs founded by Colonel Connor while relocating Morrisites from Utah.

1863: Nez Perce Reservation established.

1864: Boise City is incorporated and becomes territorial capital.

1864: John West arrives in Boise, called "Dean of Colored Pioneers in Idaho."

1865: U.S. Civil War ends, numerous refugees from Missouri and Southern states move to Idaho.
1866: Beginning of the Snake Indian War 1866-1868.
1866: Gold discovered at Leesburg.
1866: Telegraph service arrives in Idaho.
1867: Idaho repeals oath of allegiance to U.S. resulting in riots and calling out of Federal troops.
1868: Owyhee War.
1869: Transcontinental railroad completed with Idaho served by railroad points in Utah and Nevada via stage and freight lines.
1869: First telegraph line arrives at Franklin.
1869: Fort Hall Reservation established by President Grant.
1869: Placer gold found at Oro Grande.
1870: Caribou gold rush north of Soda Springs.
1872: Idaho prison completed.
1872: U.S. Assay office built in Boise
1874: First railroad service reaches Idaho at Franklin near Utah border.
1874: Owyhee Avalanche, Idaho's first daily newspaper prints.

1875: Lemhi reservation established by President Grant.
1877: Duck Valley Reservation established by President Hayes.
1877: Nez Perce and Bannock Indian Wars 1877-1878.
1883: First telephone exchange begins operation in Lewiston.
1878: Camp Coeur d'Alene established.
1879: Sheepeater Indian War.
1880: Boise and Lewiston independent school districts established.
1882: Construction on the New York Canal begins.
1882: First electric light burns at Philadelphia Smelter near Ketchum.
1882: Northern Pacific Railroad completed in Idaho.
1884: Coeur d'Alene gold rush.
1884: Freight and passenger steam boats begin on Coeur d'Alene Lake.
1884: Oregon Short Line Railroad ties Idaho to the Pacific Coast.
1884: Silver discovered near Coeur d'Alene and in Silver Valley.
1885: Bunker Hill and Sullivan mines open.

1885: Test Oath Act adopted. Bans Mormons from voting or holding public office.
1886: Territorial Capitol completed.
1888: Ricks College established at Rexburg.
1889: Hailey fire - $750,000 damage.
1889: State Constitutional Convention on July 4th. Ratified by voters November 5th.
1889: Territorial Asylum Fire in November.
1889: University of Idaho established at Moscow.
1890: Burke Snowslide.
1890: Great Northern Railroad completed through Idaho.
1890: Idaho becomes the 43rd state, signed into law by President Benjamin Harrison.
1890: George L. Shoup first governor.
1891: Boise electric streetcars begin operation.
1891: College of Idaho opens in Caldwell.
1891: Emma Edward's design for the Great Seal of the State of Idaho adopted, first and only state seal created by a woman.
1892: Coeur d'Alene labor strike.
1893: Normal Schools established at Lewiston and Albion.
1893: Panic of '93 leads to collapse of silver and lead prices, shutting down the Coeur d'Alene mines.
1893: Wagon roads established between Northern and Southern Idaho.
1894: Carey Act opens land to irrigation and settlement.
1896: Idaho gives women the right to vote.
1896: Butch Cassidy robs Montpelier bank.
1896: Range Wars result in murder of sheepherders, "Diamondfield Jack" Davis blamed.
1898: First Idaho regiment of volunteers leaves to fight in the Philippines.
1898: Fort Hall Reservation allotment of 160 acres to each resident.

1899: Coeur d'Alene labor strike and concentrator explosion.
1900: New York Canal completed.
1901: Academy of Idaho opens in Pocatello (later to become ISU).
1901: Swan Falls hydroelectric dam completed.
1902: Pocatello land rush.
1902: Reclamation Act used to build dams and canals in Idaho.
1903: Idaho Industrial Training reform school founded at St Anthony.
1903: Milner Dam on Snake River opens and transforms the Magic Valley.
1904: Humanitarian and peacemaker Chief Joseph dies.
1905: Governor Steunenberg assassination.
1905: New state capitol authorized.
1905: Twin Falls Land and Water Company established by I.B. Perrine.
1906: Minidoka Dam completed.
1906: Potlatch sawmill opens, largest in the United States.
1906: University of Idaho Admin building fire.
1907: State flag adopted.
1908: State parks established: Heyburn, Shoshone Falls, Payette Lake.
1910: North Idaho fires known as the "The Big Blowup."
1910: State highway district law enacted.
1910: The Big Burn.
1912: State Board of Education established.
1913: Northwest Nazarene College founded in Nampa.
1913: School for Deaf and Blind opens in Gooding.
1914: Moses Alexander elected, first Jewish governor in United States.
1915: Arrowrock Dam completed.

1916: State highway program established.
1916: Statewide prohibition ratified and begins January 1, 1916.
1917: Gilmore Pittsburgh Mine Explosion.
1917: State fair established at Boise.
1917: WWI.
1918: Spanish Influenza pandemic.
1919: Lava Hot Springs established as a state-operated resort.
1920: 15-year-old Philo Farnsworth creates concept behind invention of television.
1920: State Capitol completed.
1922: First licensed radio stations are KFBA in Lewiston and KFAN in Moscow on July 6. KFAU follows closely on July 18th at Boise High School.
1924: Craters of the Moon National Monument established.
1925: Union Pacific service to Boise established.
1926: First commercial airmail service in the U.S. begun in Boise. Route from Pasco, Washington, to Elko, Nevada.
1927: American Falls Dam completed.
1929: Adelyne Champers becomes first woman to argue and win a case before Idaho Supreme Court.
1931: Idaho Primitive Area established as joint decision by U.S. Forest Service and Idaho Legislature.
1931: Legislature adopts state song, official flower and state bird.
1931: State income tax adopted.
1932-33: Boise Junior College opens; North Idaho Junior College established at Coeur d'Alene.
1934: Idaho becomes first in the nation in silver production.

1935: Legislature purchases Spalding Mission as a state park.
1935: Pea Pickers Rebellion in Teton County. Martial law declared .
1935: Statewide prohibition repealed and Liquor Dispensary system developed.
1936: I.W.W. lumber strike. Martial law declared in Clearwater County.
1936: Sun Valley resort built by Union Pacific Railroad. Operates first ski chair lift in the world.
1936: William E. Borah becomes Idaho's first Presidential candidate.
1937: Nampa July fireworks explosion.
1938: Fish & Game Commission established.
1939: Idaho State Police established.
1939: Joe Albertson opens his first supermarket.
1941: Gowen Field established south of Boise as U.S. military base.
1941: JR Simplot begins potato dehydration operation.
1941: U.S. enters WWII.
1942: Farragut Naval Training Station established at Lake Pend Oreille.
1942: Japanese-Americans internment camps established.
1942: Pocatello Army Air Base, Naval Gun Plant established.

1945: J.R. Simplot opens Idaho's first phosphate processing plant.
1947: Idaho State Archives established.
1948: Bureau of Reclamation begins planning to construct Hell's Canyon Dam for flood control.
1949: National Reactor Testing Station established at Arco.
1950: State Highway Department established.
1951: EBR-1 begins operation as the first nuclear fission reactor in the world to generate electricity.
1951: State teachers' colleges at Lewiston and Albion closed.
1953: Idaho's first television station opens, KIDO-TV, Boise.
1954: Submarine reactor developed, tested, and perfected at National Reactor Testing Station.
1955: Arco Idaho becomes first community to receive electricity from a nuclear reactor.
1955: Lewis-Clark Normal school opens at Lewiston.
1956: Construction in Idaho of the National Interstate Highway System begins.
1956: Palisades Dam completed.
1959: Brownlee Dam completed.
1960: Bunker Hill Mine strike for seven months.

1961: Ernest Hemingway dies at Ketchum, July 2nd.
1961: Harriman Railroad Ranch promised to state as a state park.
1961: Oxbow Dam completed on Snake River.
1965: Nez Perce National Historic Park established.
1967: International Boy Scout Jamboree at Farragut State Park.
1968: Hell's Canyon Dam completed.
1970: National Farmers Organization caravan to Boise protesting potato prices.
1971: Idaho Penitentiary riot, $25,000 in damage.
1971: Last log drive on the Clearwater River.
1972: Sunshine Mine Disaster.
1973: Dworshak Dam completed.
1973: Les Purce is first Black elected official in Idaho. He later serves as mayor of Pocatello.
1973: Boise State College becomes Boise State University.
1974: Evel Knievel fails to complete jump over Snake River Canyon.
1974: Kootenai Indians in northern Idaho "declare war" on U.S. government to gain government recognition.
1975: New Idaho state penitentiary opens.
1975: Port of Lewiston opens making Idaho an inland sea port.
1976: Hells Canyon National Recreation Area created.
1976: Teton Dam collapse.
1980: Central Idaho Wilderness Act establishes the 2.2 million acre River of No Return Wilderness Area.
1980: Riot at Idaho State Prison, $2 million in damages.
1981: Control of jack rabbit populations creates controversy with animal protection groups.

1982: Harriman State Park dedicated.
1983: Borah Peak Earthquake.
1984: Salmon River ice jam flood.
1985: Grasshopper plague.
1985: Potlatch Corporation closes lumber mills near Lewiston.
1986: Claude Dallas escapes from Idaho State Penitentiary, captured five years later in California.
1987: Drought affects much of Idaho.
1988: Idaho citizens vote to remove prohibition against state lottery.
1989: Largest fires since 1910 burn in south central Idaho near Lowman.
1991: Kirby Dam collapses. Mining waste including arsenic, mercury, and cadmium flow into the Middle Fork of the Boise River.
1992: Fire in the state capitol results in $3.2 million damages.
1992: Linda Copple Trout first woman appointed to Idaho Supreme Court.
1992: Ruby Ridge standoff between Randy Weaver, Kevin Harris, and federal officials.
1995: North Idaho floods bring President to Idaho.
1995: Picabo Street becomes first American to win World Cup downhill skiing title.
1997: Severe flooding in Idaho. New Year's Day floods in southwest Idaho.
2000: 559,183 acres burned in forest fires.
2009: Idaho hosts the Special Olympics World Winter Games.
2012: Charlotte Fire destroys 60 homes in Pocatello in June.
2020: -First COVID-19 case confirmed in Idaho on March 13th.
2021: Idaho's longest legislative session in history lasts 311 days.

INTRODUCTION

Idaho is a land of extremes. Towering mountains, plunging canyons, burning desert, endless forests, and rolling Palouse — she's a beautiful lady but can be unforgiving to the reckless and foolish.

When Oregon Territory opened to settlement, the area that is now Idaho was an obstacle to overcome on the way to greener pastures near the coast. The Oregon Trail, wandering across the Snake River Plain, was something to be endured, not enjoyed. While the Native American tribes knew how to survive in such a place, the emigrants only saw desolation. This left much of Idaho to be settled later than the rest of the lower 48, but when gold appeared in her high mountain streams, the rush was on.

Born in the midst of the Civil War, the state developed a reputation for independent lifestyles, and tough men and women who could find a way to survive. Miners, loggers, ranchers, Native Americans, railroaders, lawmen, outlaws, farmers, and merchants forged Idaho into what she is today — the "Gem of the Mountains."

There is no place we would rather be than in Idaho smelling sweet syringa on the breeze while a bluebird sings high in the mountain trees. We love Idaho, not just because of her beauty, but because of her people. There is a directness and a quiet reserve in Idahoans who can be just as enigmatic as their mother state. Yes, history was long ago and the original stewards of the land and those who established communities are gone, but their unique culture remains. Their story deserves respect as we stride through the 21st century.

We want to thank the amazing members of the "Idaho History 1800 to Present" Facebook group. At the time of this writing the group includes over 58,700 members from every county in the state. We don't always agree, but we love you and appreciate your contributions to the best history group on social media! We would also like to thank Steven Branting and Arlen Walker for their kind and knowledgeable assistance in reviewing this work and suggesting improvements. Any remaining errors are ours.

— Justin & Skip

NATIVE AMERICAN

Logan Appany, Bannock

The Bannock are closely related to the Paiute, but live with the Shoshone on the Fort Hall Reservation in Southeast Idaho.

Photo by Benedicte Wrensted, courtesy of the Library of Congress.

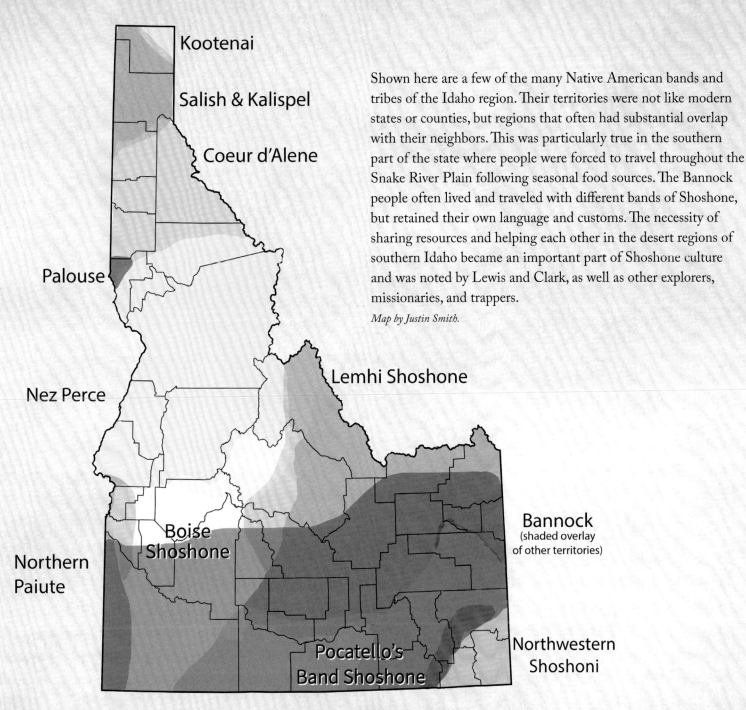

Kootenai

Salish & Kalispel

Coeur d'Alene

Palouse

Nez Perce

Lemhi Shoshone

Shown here are a few of the many Native American bands and tribes of the Idaho region. Their territories were not like modern states or counties, but regions that often had substantial overlap with their neighbors. This was particularly true in the southern part of the state where people were forced to travel throughout the Snake River Plain following seasonal food sources. The Bannock people often lived and traveled with different bands of Shoshone, but retained their own language and customs. The necessity of sharing resources and helping each other in the desert regions of southern Idaho became an important part of Shoshone culture and was noted by Lewis and Clark, as well as other explorers, missionaries, and trappers.

Map by Justin Smith.

Bannock
(shaded overlay
of other territories)

Northern
Paiute

Boise
Shoshone

Pocatello's
Band Shoshone

Northwestern
Shoshoni

Coeur d'Alene

Coeur d'Alene people, circa 1900, on the Coeur d'Alene Reservation south of Lake Coeur d'Alene. Their original territory included most of the Idaho panhandle from Lake Pend Oreille south to Orofino and east into Montana. The original reservation boundary of 1873 included all of Lake Coeur d'Alene, but during the 1880s the boundary was further reduced to its current size. *Photo by Frank Palmer.*

The Kalispel and Salish people lived near what is now the Canadian border and north of the Coeur d'Alene. They have no dedicated reservation in Idaho. This couple was photographed around 1860 by the British North American Boundary Commission.

The Kootenai homelands are at the extreme north of Idaho and cross into Canada and Montana. This group was photographed by J. R. White around 1907.

Members of the Nez Perce tribe with an Appaloosa horse, circa 1895. The Nez Perce bred the Appaloosa to be an ideal horse for riding the high mountain valleys and ridges of Central Idaho.

The Northern Paiute people are close relatives of the Bannocks and historically lived in Idaho along the borderlands with Oregon and Nevada and into California. This Charles Pierce photograph shows a Paiute woman basket weaving, circa 1900.

A Palouse-Colville family, Colville Indian Reservation, Washington, circa 1900-1910.

Photo by Edward H. Latham.

Around 1910, photographer Edward S. Curtis captured this scene of four Salish women jerking meat for storage. The Salish are also known as the Flatheads. Today, the majority of Salish live on a Montana reservation.

Chief Tindoor and his wife of the Lemhi, circa 1897

The Lemhi Shoshone lived in the mountains on the eastern portion of Idaho and north of the Snake River Plain. They were forced from their reservation to Fort Hall in 1907.

Photo by Benedicte Wrensted, courtesy of the Library of Congress.

Chief Joseph

Chief Joseph (Hinmatóowyalahtqit) of the Wallowa band of the Nez Perce led his people on an epic escape from the United States Cavalry in 1877. Forced to leave their ancestral lands for a small reservation in Idaho, Joseph and his people chose to try to make their way to Canada to seek asylum. Leading 700 men, women, and children, Joseph and his war chiefs outmaneuvered the army, traveling over 1,170 miles through Idaho and Montana. By October, with 150 of his people dead, women and children exhausted, and no hope of help in Canada, he surrendered. His speech at his surrender is one of the most moving in history:

"I am tired of fighting. Our chiefs are killed. Looking Glass is dead. Toohoolhoolzote is dead. The old men are all dead. It is the young men who say, 'Yes' or 'No.' He who led the young men is dead. It is cold, and we have no blankets. The little children are freezing to death. My people, some of them, have run away to the hills, and have no blankets, no food. No one knows where they are — perhaps freezing to death. I want to have time to look for my children, and see how many of them I can find. Maybe I shall find them among the dead. Hear me, my chiefs! I am tired. My heart is sick and sad. From where the sun now stands I will fight no more forever."

Following his surrender, the Nez Perce were moved to Fort Leavenworth, Kansas, as prisoners of war. Eight months later, the survivors were moved to Indian Territory (Oklahoma) where many died from epidemics. Their return to the Northwest was long and rife with false promises from the U.S. Government.

Photographer unknown, courtesy of Smithsonian Collections.

EXPLORERS AND TRAPPERS

On August 26, 1805, the Lewis and Clark expedition were led through Lemhi pass into what is now Idaho by a Lemhi Shoshone woman named Sacagawea. There, her brother, Chief Cameahwait, traded horses to the explorers and provided guides to lead them through the rugged mountains on their way to the Pacific.

Lewis and Clark Reach Shoshone Camp Led by Sacajawea the Bird Woman by Charles Marion Russell, 1918.

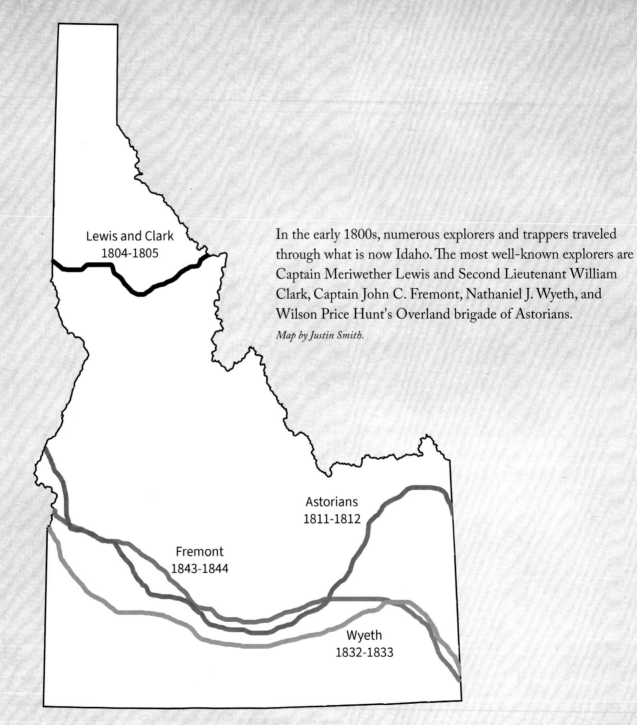

Lewis and Clark
1804-1805

In the early 1800s, numerous explorers and trappers traveled through what is now Idaho. The most well-known explorers are Captain Meriwether Lewis and Second Lieutenant William Clark, Captain John C. Fremont, Nathaniel J. Wyeth, and Wilson Price Hunt's Overland brigade of Astorians.

Map by Justin Smith.

Astorians
1811-1812

Fremont
1843-1844

Wyeth
1832-1833

Trappers

During the first half of the 19th century, the Pacific Northwest was seen as a fur trapping business opportunity for both the United States and the British Hudson's Bay Company. Outposts were staffed by employees of companies who not only trapped animals for furs, but also negotiated trade agreements with Native American tribes who exchanged furs for ammunition, firearms, and other goods. The total number of trappers who worked the region is unknown. Here are some of the most notable who trapped in what is today Idaho.

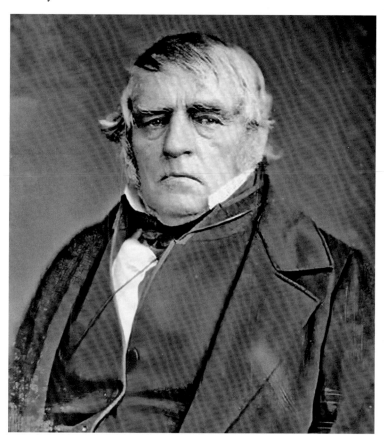

Peter Skene Ogden, Southern and Eastern Idaho.

ABOVE: Donald Mackenzie, Lewiston area and Southern Idaho.

ABOVE LEFT: Jim Bridger was an explorer, mountain man, trapper, guide, and Army scout who often visited East Idaho.

ABOVE RIGHT: Alexander Ross.

All photos courtesy of the Library of Congress.

Captain Benjamin Louis Eulalie de Bonneville brought the first covered wagons over the Rockies to the Lemhi River.

ABOVE: Kit Carson, Salmon River Country.

RIGHT: Nathaniel Wyeth established Fort Hall near present-day Pocatello.

All photos courtesy of the Library of Congress.

Mission of the Sacred Heart, locally known as the Cataldo Mission, is the oldest standing building in Idaho. Designed in 1850 by the Jesuit missionary Antonio Ravalli, it was constructed over three years by local Native Americans under Ravalli's leadership. Decoration of the interior was also undertaken by the local peoples. The church's walls are made of wattle and daub. No nails were used in the building. Today, the church is protected as part of the Coeur d'Alene's Old Mission State Park.

LEFT: Interior

Postcards courtesy of Justin Smith.

EMIGRANTS ON THE TRAILS

Three Island Crossing

The Oregon Trail was not a single wagon road, but a network of trails from Missouri to Oregon with many alternate routes. In Idaho, the emigrants generally followed the main route along the south side of the Snake River until they arrived at Three Island Crossing, where Glenns Ferry is today. Some emigrants took the shorter routes with less water north of the river including Goodale's Cutoff (originally scouted by John Jeffrey).

While the great majority of interactions between emigrants and bands of Shoshone and Bannock were peaceful (more emigrants died from diseases and accidents than from attacks from Native Americans), by the 1850s, tensions were growing. Increasing numbers of emigrants were traveling through Eastern Idaho on their way to the California gold fields using a network of cutoffs. The seemingly endless flood of wagons and livestock across the arid Snake River Plain quickly depleted the natural resources. Worse, white and Native American scoundrels would occasionally take random shots at each other. Similarly, some white bandits

Painting by William Henry Jackson.

disguised themselves as Native Americans and attacked wagon trains. Faced with fear, hostility, dwindling resources, and indifference from the U.S. Government, bloody fights broke out, including the Ward Massacre near modern-day Middleton in Canyon County.

In August of 1862, Chief Pocatello attempted a blockade of the main road of the Oregon Trail with a series of running skirmishes west of American Falls. Pocatello's band got the worst of the fighting

but succeeded in pushing some traffic to the Goodale route. California and Utah newspapers quickly labeled the fighting an "outrage" and a "massacre" by the Native Americans and demanded military action. Five months later, Col. Patrick E. Connor ordered his California Volunteers to attack a village of Northwestern Shoshoni on Bear River as retribution before bothering to attempt opening formal negotiations with the Shoshone and Bannock peoples.

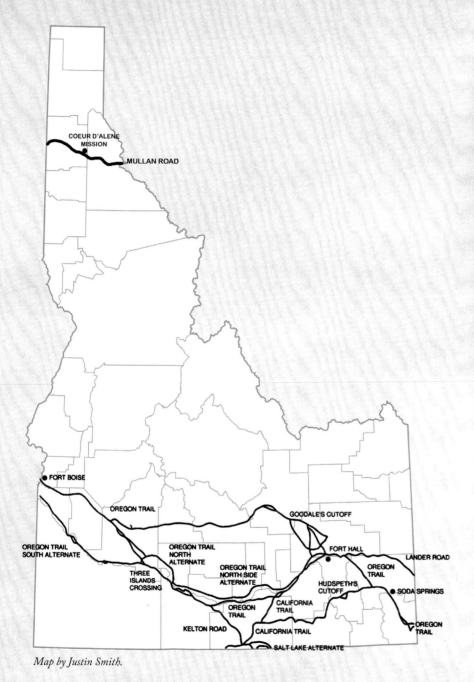

Map by Justin Smith.

The map contains the following labels:

COEUR D'ALENE MISSION

MULLAN ROAD

FORT BOISE

OREGON TRAIL

OREGON TRAIL SOUTH ALTERNATE

OREGON TRAIL NORTH ALTERNATE

THREE ISLANDS CROSSING

OREGON TRAIL NORTH SIDE ALTERNATE

OREGON TRAIL

KELTON ROAD

GOODALE'S CUTOFF

FORT HALL

HUDSPETH'S CUTOFF

CALIFORNIA TRAIL

OREGON TRAIL

LANDER ROAD

SODA SPRINGS

OREGON TRAIL

CALIFORNIA TRAIL

SALT LAKE ALTERNATE

TO THE MEMORY OF
THE PIONEERS WHO WERE
MASSACRED BY INDIANS
NEAR THIS SPOT
AUGUST 20, 1854.

THIS MONUMENT IS DEDICATED
BY
PIONEER CHAPTER

DAUGHTERS OF THE
AMERICAN REVOLUTION
BOISE, IDAHO.

WILLIAM WARD	AGE	44
MARGARET WARD	"	37
MARY WARD	"	18
ROBERT WARD	"	16
EDWARD WARD	"	9
FRANCIS WARD	"	7
FLORA WARD	"	5
SUSAN WARD	"	3
ELIZA WHITE	"	30
GEORGE WHITE	"	4
SAMUEL MALLAGAN		
CHARLES ADAMS		
WILLIAM BABCOCK		
DR. ADAMS		

AMEN
ADOLPH SCHULTZ
JOHN FREDERICK
FRENCH CANADIAN

Ward Massacre monument.

Fort Hall, located along the Oregon Trail, was one of the most important supply points on the Oregon and California Trails. It served as a fur trading post and supply post. This 1849 engraving is by Major Osborne Cross. Nothing remains of the old fort situated on the Fort Hall Indian Reservation just north of Pocatello.

Lithograph artist unknown.

RIGHT: An excellent replica of the fort stands in the southern part of Pocatello.

Photo by Justin Smith.

GOLD RUSHES AND STAGE ROADS

While gold panning stream bottom is a romantic image, the practice was typically only used by the earliest prospectors. Once good ground was found, larger operations quickly followed.

Photo courtesy of the US Forest Service.

This 1863 photo shows what may be the earliest image of the Boise Basin. The town is difficult to identify as many mining towns burned multiple times due to all-wood construction and frequent accidents.

Franklin

On April 14, 1860, a small group of Mormon Pioneers began a small settlement in northern Cache Valley, believing they were in Utah. In the early 1870s, the Hayden Survey found that Franklin (behind the large butte in the William Henry Jackson photo) was north of the 42nd parallel and thus part of Idaho, making it the first and oldest permanent settlement in Idaho today. While the Mormon's primary goal was to establish farming, in July of 1862 they found themselves along the easiest route from Salt Lake City to the gold mines at Grasshopper Creek in present-day Montana. The ongoing north-south traffic caused significant problems for the Shoshone people who called Cache Valley their home.

Photo possibly by William Henry Jackson, Hayden Expedition.

Pierce

Prior to 1860, what is now known as Idaho was considered an empty wilderness and an impediment to reaching the West Coast. The Oregon Trail through the southern portion of the state, as well as the California Trail breaking off of the Oregon Trail at Raft River, west of American Falls, and the new Mullan Trail were all designed to facilitate travel through the wilderness as quickly as possible. However, on October 2, 1860, Captain E.D. Pierce made the first Idaho gold discovery on Orofino Creek. Pierce wrote, "we moved down and camped on the stream, afterwards called Oraphenia creek. Here we found better prospects than further up the stream where we first made the discovery, which was a sufficient guarantee that we had a rich and extensive mining camp, and organized a new mining district, and gave its boundaries, drafted a code of mining laws, to govern our new mining district."

The town of Pierce (shown here in 1905) bears his name and is home to Shoshone County's first courthouse and Idaho's oldest public building. It still stands on its original location in Pierce.

Captain E.D. Pierce.

Courthouse.

Photo by James E. Babb.

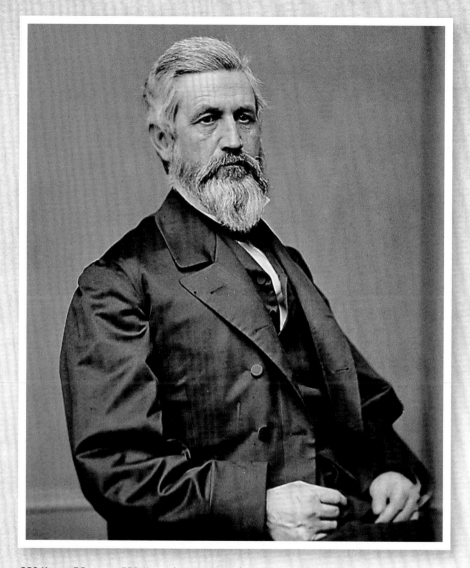

William Henson Wallace (1811–1879) was appointed the first governor of Idaho Territory by Abraham Lincoln. He also served as Congressional delegate from both Washington Territory and Idaho Territory. After being elected as delegate for Idaho Territory, he vacated his gubernatorial appointment, serving for only part of one year.

Placer Mines, Delta.
Photo courtesy of Thomas N. Barnard Studio, Barnard-Stockbridge Photograph Collection, University of Idaho.

The easiest gold to find was typically discovered as flakes and nuggets in streambeds. Panning for gold by hand was the cheapest way to separate the deposits from sand or gravel. Once a stream with a good amount of gold was found, the miners worked upstream to determine where the gold originated. Often large gravel bars were found filled with the precious metal. Miners used hydraulic Monitors (water cannons) to blast the gravel out of the hillside and into sluices where it could be washed to extract the gold.

Caleb Lyon was appointed territorial governor by President Lincoln following the resignation of William Wallace. However, Lyon was far from a stellar choice. He spent most of his career jumping from one political position to another. As governor of Idaho, he was the driving force behind moving the capital from Lewiston to Boise, a task he accomplished using no small amount of political subterfuge. He also started a false claim of diamonds being found in Idaho, resulting in a rush to Ruby City. As a final act, he stole $46,418 of federal funds earmarked for the Nez Perce. After leaving Idaho, he returned to his native New York where he built a mansion with his ill-gotten gains.

When the gold rush to Boise Basin began in 1862, miners panned every stream and checked every quartz vein in the region. More often than not they struck gold. Soon businesses followed to "mine the miners" and towns such as Placerville, Pioneerville, and Centerville emerged. Thousands of people moved to the Basin to find their fortune. One such town was founded in 1862 and named Bannock. However, when Idaho Territory was first formed, the people of Bannock in the Boise Basin and the people of Bannock in what is now Montana often found their mail going to the wrong place. The residents began calling one town West Bannock and the other East Bannock. Eventually, the territorial legislature solved the confusion by renaming West Bannock, at the confluence of Elk and Mores Creeks, as Idaho City. Across the placer tailings was Buena Vista Bar and both communities grew rapidly. The first miners panned for gold, but they soon realized the placer deposits in the valley bottoms were full of gold. Hydraulic mining began that eventually led to dredges which literally turned the valley floor upside down to wash out the gold.

So much wealth made the Boise Basin into a Wild West town. Shootings, hurdy-gurdy girls, hangings, claim jumping, and multiple fires punctuated the city's boom times. Today, Idaho City remains a lively little town with much of that Old West feel. The gold is nearly all gone, but the signs of the 1860s rush are everywhere in dredge tailings, ponds, and other artifacts of the past.

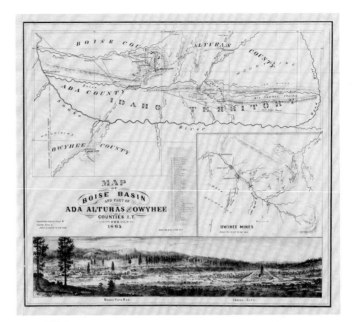

RIGHT: First dredge, Idaho City

When gold and silver were discovered on War Eagle Mountain in 1864, miners raced to the Owyhee Mountains to hunt for the glittering metals near the 8,065-foot peak. Dewey (Boonville), Ruby City, De Lamar, Wagontown, and other small communities dotted the mountain, but eventually Silver City became the grandest of them all and served as the county seat beginning in 1867.

A $70,000 stamp mill was built to serve the mines and in just 45 days bettered that initial investment when it recovered $90,000 in silver and gold. Idaho's first daily newspaper and telegraph office quickly followed. Miners and businessmen often traveled the stage road between Silver City, Boise, and Idaho City during the early years.

Companies competed for the silver, and in September 1865 armed conflict broke out from rivalry over the Poorman vein. However, it was the Owyhee War in March of 1868 that pitted the Golden Chariot and the Ida Elmore mines against each other, resulting in gunfire between the miners inside the mountain tunnels.

Hired gunmen were brought in, and each side armed themselves for steadily increasing conflict. Over 100 men were involved in the fight before Governor Ballard sent in the military to stop the shooting. Four days later the fight was over.

Silver City was an immensely rich mining town and one of the first towns in Idaho with electricity and telephone service, but when the mines waned in the 1890s the city went into a slow decline. Today the city's remaining buildings are carefully preserved by the residents who still live over a mile high in the Owyhee Mountains.

TOP: Hydraulic mining near the Boise River.

ABOVE: Extensive mine works at Idaho City.

—ATLANTA MINE—
ATLANTA IDAHO.

Situated 35 miles east of Idaho City, Atlanta was founded as a mining camp in November of 1864. The gold and silver mines were named by hopeful southerners who heard a rumor of a Confederate victory over General Sherman in Atlanta, Georgia. The rumor turned out to be false, but the name stuck.

Lithograph by Edmond Greene.

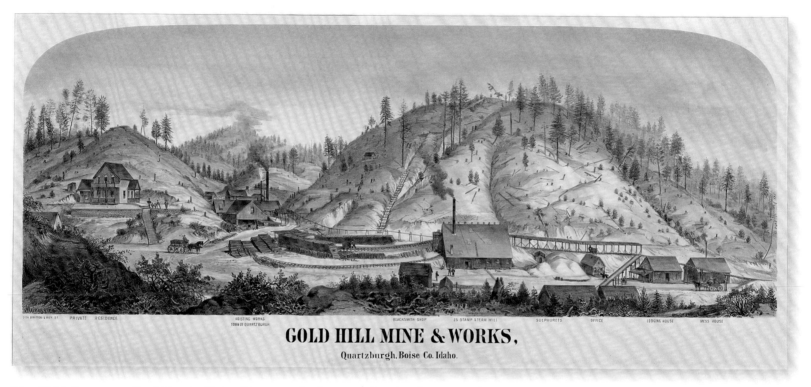

GOLD HILL MINE & WORKS,
Quartzburgh, Boise Co. Idaho.

The 1862 discovery of gold in the Boise Basin resulted in a mad rush of miners, saloon keepers, merchants, hurdy-gurdy girls, and anyone else who thought they could make money from the gold bonanza. Shortly after the rush began, miners discovered a gold-bearing vein of quartz northwest of Placerville. A blacksmith, stamp mill, and boarding house soon appeared.

Lithograph by Edmond Greene.

Taylor's Bridge

When gold was discovered in what is now Eastern Idaho and Montana, large quantities of supplies had to be freighted from Salt Lake in massive freight wagons chained together and pulled by oxen. However, crossing the Snake River on a ferry was a difficult task even when the water was low. Seizing an opportunity, in 1865 James Madison Taylor built one of Idaho's first toll bridges where the river narrows significantly. Taylor's crossing soon took the name Eagle Rock and a community developed around the bridge. That community is now known as Idaho Falls.

Photo by William Henry Jackson, 1871.

Boise City, Idaho Territory, c. 1870

Boise City was incorporated in 1864 next to the new Fort Boise, placed at the crossroads of the Oregon Trail and the Silver City to Boise Basin road. The fort and the heavy traffic through the area made the location important to all of southwestern Idaho. The next year, the capital of the territory was moved from Lewiston to Boise.

Idaho State Penitentiary

The old Idaho State Penitentiary in Boise opened in 1872 and for 101 years housed the worst criminals Idaho had to offer. Escapes and riots kept the warden and guards on their toes. Bloodhounds were put to good use chasing criminals who went over the wall. The prison was finally replaced after inmates rioted over poor living conditions in 1973. Today it serves as a museum operated by the Idaho State Historical Society.

Photos courtesy of the Idaho State Historical Society.

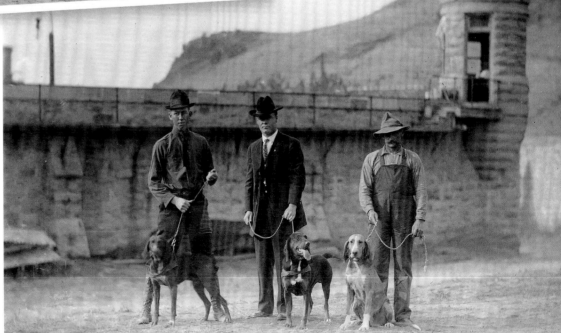

Burke

Discovery of lead and silver in Burke Canyon in 1884 resulted in one of the most unique towns ever built in North America. Shoe-horned into the bottom of the canyon, Burke had only one street shared by wagons and two railroads. At the end of town was the 150-room Tiger Hotel; space was so tight that the railway had to run through the lobby. This view is circa 1891.

Lewiston, Washington Territory, August 1862

Established in 1861, Lewiston was built at the confluence of the Snake and Clearwater rivers to serve as a supply point for the gold rush in the Florence Basin. The city was named the Idaho Territory's capital in 1863 when the territory was formed. However, in 1865, the capital was permanently moved to Boise, due in part to political fighting as well as the rapid move of many miners to the new Boise Basin mines. Lewiston's advantageous position secured the future of the town, which today is Idaho's only seaport.

Photo by Edward D. Sammis.

ABOVE: Northern Idaho was the site of a fleet of steamboats that traveled up and down the Columbia River and docked at Lewiston. Other steamboats were used on lakes near Coeur d'Alene for passenger and freight transportation. The *Lewiston*, shown here, was owned by Union Pacific Railroad as an extension of their freight operations from Oregon. The last steamboat left Lewiston in 1940.

RAILROADS

U&N Bridge

The first railroad bridge in Idaho was placed across the Bear River in 1878, just north of modern-day Preston in the southeastern corner of the state. Built by the Utah & Northern Railway (formerly the Utah Northern Railroad), it crossed the river near the site of the 1863 massacre of Shoshone by the California Volunteers. The U&N built a roundhouse and shops on the north side of the river and named the new town Battle Creek after the site of the massacre. For a while, it was the largest town in the area, but when the railroad moved the shops to Eagle Rock the town quickly began to dwindle, and Preston began to grow as a farming community.

Photo by Justin Smith.

Pocatello Roundhouse

Pocatello was born a railroad town and became one of the most important points on the Union Pacific system. Its immense roundhouse and workshops repaired, serviced, and rebuilt locomotives and rail cars. Shown here with approximately 30 stalls, the roundhouse would expand to almost a full circle by WWII. The large building behind it is the "back shop" where specialized and major repairs were conducted. The railroad line leading from the right side and off into the distance is the main line to Montana.

Pocatello land rush

When the Union Pacific acquired the land for Pocatello Junction, it set off a chain of events that would culminate in a large land cessation by the Shoshone-Bannock tribes and the birth of the city of Pocatello. The townsite came first by an Act of Congress in 1889. However, the most exciting event occurred on June 17, 1902, when Idaho experienced a wild land rush. A total of 418,000 acres was made available through the land cession, and all of it was for sale at bargain prices. On June 17, when the railroad shop whistle cried out at noon, the run was on with thousands of rushers and spectators crowding into the valley. The prospective settlers raced across the valley floor to stake a claim and then catch the special train to Blackfoot to file their claims. The rush had all the features of other land rushes, including those opportunists who skirted the rules. Despite the efforts of the Fort Hall Indian Agency's policemen, the illegal activities of liars and cheaters resulted in years of constant work for lawyers to resolve.

American Falls Bridge

The first major bridge of the Oregon Short Line crossed above the roaring American Falls in East Idaho in 1883. The rough and tumble construction camps were the scenes of nightly drunken revelry where gunfire was common, albeit rarely hitting more than a lit lamp or two. However, at American Falls, when two outlaws named Tex and Johnson refused orders to leave, they were summarily hanged from the partially completed bridge as a warning to others that the locals would only put up with so much.

Avery Roundhouse

Avery, Idaho, sits on the St. Joe River in Shoshone County. From 1909 to 1980, it served as a major division point on the Chicago, Milwaukee, St. Paul, and Pacific Railroad ("Milwaukee Road"). Unlike other Idaho railroads, the Milwaukee Road was partially electrified. At Avery, the trains would trade out electric locomotives, powered by overhead wires, with steam locomotives (and later diesel electrics). The tunnels and grades of the Milwaukee Road in Idaho remain as a rail trail used by bicyclists and hikers.

Eagle Rock

After passing through the Fort Hall Indian Reservation, the narrow gauge Utah & Northern Railway proceeded north until it reached Eagle Rock (present-day Idaho Falls). There the railroad built a division point with a large roundhouse, shops, and a bridge near Taylor's Bridge, crossing the narrow black canyon of the Snake River. However, after a labor dispute and a windstorm that blew down the roundhouse, the railroad moved the shops to Pocatello Junction to better serve both the U&N and the Oregon Short Line. Eagle Rock suffered a near total loss of its population, recovering only when irrigation brought water to the fertile Snake River Plain, after which residents renamed it Idaho Falls.

Photo by C.R. Savage.

Nampa

When the Oregon Short Line arrived in the Treasure Valley, the locals assumed it would divert to the capital at Boise. However, land speculators tried to force the railroad to pay exorbitant prices for lots along the approach. Rather than pay the extra cost, the railroad bypassed the capital and built stations at Kuna and Nampa in 1883. In subsequent years, the railroad added more railroad shops and a roundhouse at the newly founded town of Nampa. For years afterward Boiseans were forced to take a long wagon ride to Kuna to catch the train at the nearest depot. However, Nampa grew rapidly and remained an important point for the Oregon Short Line.

TOP LEFT: Nampa Depot.

TOP RIGHT: Coaling station at Nampa.
Photo by Russell Lee, 1941, courtesy of the Library of Congress.

PANORAMA: Nampa, circa 1907.
Photo by Russell Lee, courtesy of the Library of Congress.

Boise

Boise's frustration at being bypassed by the railroad became a major point of contention for its citizens. The railroad was the only efficient means of long distance transportation, and a capital city without a depot was simply unacceptable! In 1887, the railroad finally built a spur to the bench above Boise near the location of the present depot. However, the townspeople were still unhappy with the arrangement. The depot was a mile outside of town, on the south side of the Boise River, and up a steep slope. Boise's political and business leaders continued to fight for a depot in the city. That was finally accomplished when the second depot was built in 1893 at 10th and Front Streets. A separate freight depot was also built along Front Street. It was not until 1925 that Boise's iconic depot (back up on the bench) was built and dedicated. Thousands turned out to celebrate the long-awaited arrival of through train service in Boise.

TOP: First Boise depot.

MIDDLE: Second depot on Front Street.

RIGHT: Crowds at opening of the third depot.

Lewiston and Grangeville

Lewiston faced its own unique challenges when rail service finally arrived. The Camas Prairie Railroad operated by Lewiston and Grangeville was an engineering marvel with soaring bridges over canyons and seven tunnels blasted through the walls of a canyon to create a climbable grade for the steam locomotives. Completed in 1908, the Union Pacific and Northern Pacific jointly operated the line to provide service to the small towns of the Camas Prairie. Lewiston was provided with freight and passenger rail, as well as a trolley system that included service across the Snake River to Clarkston, Washington.

TOP LEFT: Tunnel Number 1 Lewiston-Grangeville Line.
Photo by Lillian M. Bell.

TOP RIGHT: Opening of the Clearwater train bridge at Lewiston, July 7, 1908.

LEFT: Steel bridge over Lawyers Canyon, 1908.

Treasure Valley Interurban

Operating from 1891-1928, Treasure Valley's streetcar system was by far the largest in Idaho. The Boise Traction Company operated a long-looped track from Boise to Caldwell, Nampa, Meridian, and back again to Boise. The electric trolleys were operated with electricity from Swan Falls, Salmon Falls, and Shoshone Falls. Old tracks are still occasionally uncovered by road crews in Boise, reminding older residents of the trolleys that passed by the Idanha Hotel (above) and stopped at the depot across from the Capitol Building. While the trolleys no longer run through the valley, portions of the company still remain in business as part of the Idaho Power Company, most notably the hydroelectric operations that first powered the street cars.

Ferries

The earliest ferries in Idaho were on the Clearwater and Snake Rivers to serve gold miners in Idaho and what would become Montana. The operators took great care to place their ferries at the perfect location to exploit traffic throughout the year. Some towns and villages today recall those old businesses with names like Bonners Ferry and Glenns Ferry. While travel was greatly aided by the arrival of the railroads, livestock, and eventually cars still had to find their way from one side of the river to another until suitable bridges could be built. Likely the most exciting ferry was operated just above Shoshone Falls, where the water plunged a dizzying 212 feet into the Snake River Canyon. Ferries were usually safe, but a broken cable sent at least one of the ferries over the falls along with everyone aboard.

Photo by Grove Karl Gilbert, Harriman Expedition, May 1899.

RECLAMATION AND HYDROPOWER

Spalding and Lemhi Missions

The first recorded irrigation in Idaho occurred at the Spalding Mission in the Lapwai Valley in 1839, when Henry Spalding dug a ditch to try to save his crops. Another mission at Kamiah also dug a ditch that year, but anything like a true farm was to wait until 1855 when the Mormon Salmon River Mission in the Lemhi Valley was established. Fort Lemhi (originally spelled Limhi) closed only three years later after a dispute with the local Bannock and Shoshone bands. After the Mormons departed, the old fort continued to be used as a farm to provide produce to miners on the east side of the mountains in what is now Montana. Similar farms were begun in other regions of Idaho to provide a source of food for hungry miners working high in the mountains. The ditch dug by the Mormons in the Lemhi Valley still carries water today. Another Mormon settlement at Franklin in the Cache Valley also owes its existence to irrigation. Established in 1860, it remains Idaho's oldest town and nearby farms continue to operate utilizing irrigation from nearby streams and the Cub River.

TOP RIGHT: The remains of a Spalding Mission cabin.

MIDDLE LEFT: Dr. Henry Spalding.

MIDDLE RIGHT: Eliza Spalding.

Notably, the Spaldings had another historical first when they operated the first printing press in the Pacific Northwest as part of their missionary work. Spalding also constructed a water-powered saw mill and grist mill in 1840.

Treasure Valley reclamation

The gold rush to the Boise Basin brought thousands of miners to the region and prices for goods skyrocketed. In the first few years, freighters hauled food and other supplies from Oregon to the mining camps and towns. Paper money was frowned upon, with nearly all transactions conducted in gold dust. It was not long before farms, lumber mills, and grist mills sprouted along the Boise River near the new capital.

As the city grew along with the military post at Fort Boise, all of the land near the river and streams was quickly claimed. The farmers knew the valley floor was covered in rich soil; they formed canal companies to divert water out of the rivers and streams and into their fields.

The Ridenbaugh and New York Canals both began operation this way. However, canal companies ran into numerous financial problems, and it was not until the Carey Act in 1894 that the United States government stepped in and assisted with the projects. In the early 1900s, new canal projects opened near Caldwell (Pioneer Irrigation District) and elsewhere in the Treasure Valley. The New York Canal was greatly expanded in 1910 and still serves as a primary irrigation source in the valley today.

Construction of the New York Canal.

All photos courtesy of US Reclamation Service, Bureau of Reclamation, 1910.

Magic Valley

The Magic Valley transformation was truly impressive by any standard. What had been sagebrush desert trodden by emigrants on the Oregon Trail turned into lush fields, small farming hamlets, and cities. Buildings like the Riverside Inn at Milner capitalized on the town's birth as the mighty Snake River was captured and tamed. The three-storey grand hotel boasted all the modern comforts including plumbing and electricity. Steam tractors, such as the one operated by Clarence Bisbee of Twin Falls and shown on the opposite page, hauled freight to Salmon Falls Creek and other locations in the valley.

Stagecoach, Twin Falls, 1910.

By 1918, C.J. Brosnan published this map in his History of the State of Idaho showing the extensive irrigation projects not only in the Magic Valley (bottom center of map), but also in the Upper Snake River, Treasure, Lemhi, Lost River, Bear River, and Payette valleys. Today travelers driving the freeway from Idaho Falls to Boise witness seemingly endless fields of grain, potatoes, sugar beets, and other crops thriving in the rich volcanic soil. Cropland is irrigated by Idaho's rivers and the enormous Upper Snake River Plain aquifer that breaks free from the Snake River Canyon's wall at Thousand Springs.

ABOVE: Tractor engine starting from Twin Falls to Salmon River Dam, 1908.

Photo by Clarence Bisbee.

LEFT: Riverside Inn at Milner.

American Falls

No portion of the Snake River in Idaho has seen more continuous development over its history than at American Falls. The initial railroad bridge over the falls was an amazing achievement that gave travelers a thrill as the train crossed the roaring waters. It was not long before business leader (and later governor) James Brady deduced that the falling water could be used to provide electricity to Pocatello and other nearby towns. In 1901, his American Falls Power, Water and Light Company began construction of a power plant on the island in the middle of the falls. Water was diverted to the turbines by a weir (a low head dam). A competing company soon began construction of another power plant on the west side of the falls.

In 1913, a third power house was planned and built on the east side of the falls. The weir was enlarged into a giant horseshoe that pushed water to both the west side and east side plants. The east side plant was further enlarged in 1924 and 1936.

TOP: First impoundment dam.

RIGHT: Center Island Power House.

LEFT: East Side Plant.

BOTTOM LEFT: Old American Falls townsite.

BOTTOM RIGHT: West side plant (on extreme left) and Center Island plant.

All photos courtesy of WaterArchives.org.

AMERICAN FALLS, IDAHO. 1926

LAKE OVER BURIED CITY, AMERICAN FALLS DAM, 1927

In 1925, the Bureau of Reclamation began construction of an impoundment dam across the Snake River that would create the enormous American Falls Reservoir. At that time, the central power plant was removed from service, but the building was left standing on the central island. Power generation continued at the much larger east side plant.

The newly created reservoir raised the level of the Snake River for 17 miles upstream. The area included a number of small villages and the city of American Falls situated just upstream from the waterfalls. As part of the project, the federal government purchased the land to be flooded, and paid to relocate houses, churches and businesses to higher ground. A new northern section of American Falls was laid out with large parks and a centrally located downtown.

Unfortunately, the concrete used in the 1925 dam was flawed, forcing the dam to be replaced. In 1978, a new dam was built just downstream from the 1925 structure. At 104 feet high and 5,277 wide, it now holds back 1,672,590 acre-feet of water. The new dam integrates with Idaho Power Company's power plant, which produces 112,420 kilowatts of electricity.

The Minidoka Dam was the first dam built by the Reclamation Service in Idaho and the first of a series of dams and canals that transformed large areas of sagebrush desert into productive farmland. Power generation was added to the design to lift water to the south side of the river. Excess electricity was distributed to nearby farmers and villages. Begun in 1904, the Minidoka Project was so successful that the region in south central Idaho was called "The Magic Valley" after farmers were able to grow produce the first full year after they cleared the land.

Photo courtesy of WaterArchives.org.

In 1915, the Bureau of Reclamation completed what was then the largest dam in the world. At 350 feet high and 1,150 feet wide, the towering dam holds back over 300,000 acre feet of water on the Boise River for irrigation use. Over the course of 30 months of construction, 527,300 cubic yards of concrete was made at a rate of 2,000 barrels a day. The government even operated its own railroad (the first ever fully operated by the Federal Government) between Barber and Arrowrock. A "work camp" was built that housed 1,400 people. The site included electric lights, central heating, and a sewage system, as well as a school, YMCA, hotel, and hospital.

Idaho Falls

Idaho Falls (originally Eagle Rock) began as nothing more than a toll bridge across the narrow black rock canyon of the Snake River in the upper valley. The arrival of the railroad in 1878 resulted in a boom that went bust in 1887 as soon as the railroad moved its division shops to Pocatello.

The small town of Eagle Rock seemed destined to die, but in 1891, a group of developers knew the rich volcanic soil in the area

ABOVE: Railroad bridge at Eagle Rock.

Photo by William Henry Jackson.

Photo courtesy of WaterArchives.org.

was ideal for farming. They had also witnessed the splendid results of irrigation from nearby Willow Creek. It was suggested that farmers did not particularly like rocks or eagles and that the town should be renamed to encourage settlement. In 1891, town leaders changed the name to Idaho Falls in reference to a series of rapids near the bridges.

In 1895, the Great Feeder began operation. What was then billed as the largest irrigation canal in the world diverted water from the Snake River to tens of thousands of acres of desert. The plucky town was not content simply with irrigation. A municipal water system was constructed to provide electrical power to the city and neighboring towns. A diversion dam above the rapids pooled water high enough to fill an old river channel on the east side of the river so it could enter the new city-operated hydroelectric plant. It had the added benefit of turning the rapids into a broad waterfall.

Teton Dam Collapse

On September 7, 1964, Congress authorized the Teton Basin Project. The project was intended to provide flood control, fish and wildlife conservation, recreation, electricity, and irrigation to the region between Teton and Rexburg in the Upper Valley. Backed by powerful interests, the location of the dam in the Teton River Narrows, just three miles northeast of Newdale, was ill-advised and destined for catastrophe.

Completed in November 1975, the reservoir created by the earthen dam quickly began to fill at a rate of about one foot per day. Five months later, the spring runoff was much higher than expected, and the project engineer requested permission to double the filling rate. Monitoring showed that ground water was filtering too quickly around the dam via large fissures in the rock that the construction company had attempted to fill with grout. One month later the fill rate was again doubled.

On June 3 and 4, springs were detected below the dam, caused by groundwater moving more than a thousand times what was originally anticipated. In addition, because the main outlet works and spillway gates were not ready yet for service, the new dam's only method for controlling its near capacity of water was the emergency outlet works.

At 7:30 a.m. on June 5, a leak appeared on the northwest face of the dam. By 9:30 a.m., the leak was releasing water up to 30 cubic feet a second. A bulldozer was sent to try to seal the leak but was unable to stem the inevitable disaster. At 11:15 a.m., a warning went out that the dam was going to fail. Crews fled the site, and at 11:55 a.m. the crest of the dam collapsed. Not long after, the remainder of the dam wall disappeared in a torrent of water.

The water poured out at over 2,000,000 cubic feet per second, raced down the canyon, and spread out across the open plain, flooding nearby villages and the city of Rexburg. By 8:00 p.m. the entire reservoir was empty.

Rising waters

The city of Rexburg was hit by multiple disasters at once. The waters flooded the streets but also crashed into a lumber yard. The lumber, in turn, ran into a fuel station, resulting in broken fuel tanks. Electrical shorts caused sparks which ignited the fuel slick, adding fire to the rapidly spreading flood. Homes floated off their foundations, railroad tracks were torn up and twisted by the rushing water, and livestock floundered and suffocated in the mud. Small farming villages simply ceased to exist.

The alert sent out by the sheriff at 11:15 a.m. came just in time for many Idahoans further downstream. Idaho Falls crews raced to sandbag the river as the waters rose. Eventually, road crews tore up the road beside bridges to allow water to flow around the structures. Further downstream at American Falls, concerns grew as water managers realized the additional water might cause more stress on the old dam with faulty concrete. Fortunately, the enormous size of the American Falls reservoir and the amount of water that flowed out onto the plain prevented a second even more devastating dam collapse.

Ultimately, 11 people died in the flood waters and the federal government was forced to pay over $300 million in damage claims. However, the actual cost of damage was much more than what the government paid out.

TOP: Rexburg.

BOTTOM: Wilford.

All photos courtesy of WaterArchives.org.

Grace Dam

While the larger dams along the Snake River are best known, numerous other small dams and reservoirs exist throughout Idaho. These dams help control seasonal flooding, provide irrigation to farmers and ranchers, and supply inexpensive electricity to nearby residents.

The Grace Dam Hydroelectric Power Plant at Grace in Caribou County is typical of these smaller dams. It is one of three hydroelectric power plants owned and operated by PacificCorp on the Bear River. Originally built in 1906-1907, the dam was upgraded in 1951 and provides 33 megawatts of electricity. The sister dams at Soda Springs and the Oneida reservoir dam provide another 44 megawatts of power while also assisting with irrigation.

COMMERCE AND EMPIRE

The spectacular Snake River Canyon running through south central Idaho was a massive obstacle to transportation, forcing traffic to scale canyon walls or travel significant distances to go around the gorge. Two soaring bridges were the solution, one near I.B. Perrine's ranch at Blue Lakes and the other eight miles further upstream. The bridge near Blue Lakes was called the Twin Falls-Jerome Bridge when it opened in 1927, but the name Perrine Bridge was soon commonly used. At 476 feet high and 1,400 feet long, it is an astonishing sight and was for a time the highest bridge in the world.

Boise City

Boise City had its beginnings in 1863 along the Oregon Trail as a military town serving the soldiers at the new Fort Boise (40 miles east of the original Fort Boise on the Snake River near Parma). With the rapid move of miners into the Boise Basin and the Owyhees, it naturally became an important supply point for both regions. Seemingly overnight, the city began to boom. The early city looked much like a Western movie set with covered wagons, hotels, saloons, and various other enterprises.

With its position as the capital guaranteed by the Territorial Supreme Court, business flourished. The Idanha Hotel rose over Main Street and was well-known as one of the finest hotels in the West. Businesses of every description opened. A thriving Basque community flourished, and immigrant miners from China established a large Chinatown.

LEFT: The Idanha Hotel.

Photo by Duane Garrett, 1974, courtesy of the Library of Congress.

Between Idaho and Main streets, just over two blocks from the Capitol, Levy's Alley housed the city's brothels.

One of the stateliest buildings was the Natatorium, a health and bathing resort placed over hot springs to the east of the city not far from the new State Penitentiary. With its soaring towers, warm waters, beautiful wood interior, and rock diving wall, it was a tourist attraction that most visitors to the city had to experience and enjoy. Today, many of the buildings in that part of the city continue to benefit from low cost geothermal heating.

TOP RIGHT: The Natatorium.

BOTTOM RIGHT: Boise Barracks.

Photo by C.R. Savage.

LEFT: Union Pacific's *Lewiston*.

BELOW: Lewiston docks.

Photo courtesy of National Archives and Records Administration, 1930.

Lewiston

Lewiston was the original capital of the Idaho Territory, ideally situated at the confluence of the Snake and Clearwater Rivers. As mining interests entered the region, the low land around the point of the two rivers became a natural place to disembark from boats. Businesses quickly set up shop, supplied by the regular arrival of steamboats that made their way up the Columbia and Snake rivers to dock along the city's westside wharf.

Lewiston grew rapidly and was rightly proud of the economic powerhouse it was becoming in the region. All commerce from the mines flowed through her ports. Ferries operated on the rivers until railroad and wagon bridges provided access to the opposite banks.

Despite losing the capital to Boise, the city continued to grow and thrive. It even spurred the birth of suburbs across the Snake River in Washington. Beautiful churches appeared at street intersections and a streetcar service ran through the town and across the bridge to Clarkston, Washington.

After Lewiston State Normal School (now Lewis-Clark State College) opened in 1896 on the bench above the original city, residents quickly began erecting spacious Queen Anne, Foursquare and Bungalow homes.

LEFT: Main Street, Lewiston circa 1918.

ABOVE RIGHT: Luna House Hotel, circa 1870.

BELOW RIGHT: The steamboat *Spokane*, circa 1905.

Pocatello

Pocatello was born as a railroad town and proudly retains that blue-collar status. Businesses mushroomed almost as soon as land for the townsite was obtained from the Fort Hall Indian Reservation. The first stone building went up along Center and Cleveland streets, with Cleveland later renamed Main. Warehouses were built near the tracks, and soon a brewery and other businesses appeared to take advantage of the rail traffic heading north to Montana, west to Oregon, south to Utah, and east to Wyoming.

Most of the original railroad housing remained, but the flimsy shacks some workers and businesses lived in were moved off the right-of-way. Small houses appeared on both the east and west side of the tracks. Pocatello House opened on the east side of the tracks to compete directly against the railroad-operated Pacific Hotel.

ABOVE: First Ford cars arrive in Pocatello.

TOP RIGHT: West Center.

BOTTOM RIGHT: Old Town from Center Street Viaduct.

In 1892, the citizens determined that a school was needed and built the first section of what is now Pocatello High School. Enterprising businessman and politician Daniel Swineheart built the city's first hydroelectric plant on the Portneuf River.

The railroad brought immense prosperity to the fledgling city. The massive railroad shops, Pacific Hotel, and large wood depot in the center of town left no question as to why Pocatello existed. The railroad operations grew as the years went by and were nothing less than a city within a city, boasting its own water system, fire department, and police force. As the fortunes of the mighty Union Pacific grew, so did the fortunes of Pocatello through much of its history.

Photo by C.R. Savage.

Blackfoot

Before there was a Pocatello Junction, Blackfoot was a primary city of Eastern Idaho. Stationed just north of the Fort Hall Indian Reservation, the city was a natural trade location and railroad stop for the Utah & Northern.

Early in its history, Blackfoot was little more than sagebrush and sand, but a women's association took it upon themselves to beautify the city through civic projects, such as planting trees. As Pocatello grew, the two cities competed economically, politically, and even on the baseball field.

Silver Valley and the Big Burn

While gold brought the first miners to Idaho, in Northern Idaho near Coeur d'Alene, it was the Silver Valley that drove the economic engine into the 20th century. The cities of Kellogg and Wallace became the center of massive mining companies and businesses that served the men and women who worked deep beneath the earth to extract the gray metal. Other small towns sprouted around Kellogg and Wallace, including Smelterville, Wardner, and Mullan.

When gold and silver were found in the 1870s, the century of mining was set into motion. Railroads snaked into the Idaho mountains as early as 1883 to haul the precious cargo and supplies in and out of the Silver Valley. Motivated by profits, large mining corporations were often at odds with their workers.

In 1892, a Pinkerton agent sent to spy on the labor union resulted in a shooting war

that left six dead and dozens injured in Burke Canyon. Similarly, in a labor dispute in 1899, miners hijacked a train, loaded it with explosives, and drove it to the Bunker Hill mine near Wardner. They used 3,000 pounds of dynamite to destroy the mill. Both uprisings resulted in the Idaho governor declaring martial law and sending troops to the valley to restore order.

The tightly packed valley experienced other disasters too. Floods and avalanches were so common that they were rarely reported outside the region unless someone died or a major mine suffered a significant loss.

In August 1910, a truly massive natural disaster

TOP: Sullivan Smelter, Wallace.

Photo courtesy of Barnard Studio, Barnard-Stockbridge Collection, University of Idaho.

ABOVE: Cedar Street, Wallace.

struck northern Idaho. Wildfires caused by lightning strikes and the embers and sparks from locomotives swept through forests in Idaho, Montana, and Washington. Backfires lit by fire crews fighting the smaller fires contributed to the blaze which smoldered into the third week of the month. On August 20, hurricane-force winds created perfect conditions for the largest wildfire in American history. The small fires converged and consumed the tinder-dry fuel built up in the forests, and over three million acres went up in smoke. The towns of Wallace, Kellogg, Osburn, Burke, and Murray were all damaged or destroyed by the raging inferno. Both Falcon and Grand Forks, Idaho, were entirely incinerated.

Thousands of men were brought in to combat the fires, but the smoke continued to rise and was visible as far east as Watertown, New York, and south as far as Dallas. When the blaze turned back on the

men, many narrowly escaped. Seventy-eight firefighters lost their lives.

Approximately one-third of Wallace was decimated, resulting in over a million dollars in damage. Trains were used to evacuate the town, while the fire crews struggled to save as many buildings as they could. Soon the town's water supply was contaminated, and firefighters commandeered beer from the local brewery to quench their thirst, until the brewery also caught fire.

The fires of 1910 became known as The Big Burn or the Big Blowup and transformed how America managed its forests and fires, with a new emphasis on fighting all fires as quickly as possible.

OPPOSITE PAGE: Downtown Wallace after the 1910 fire.

ABOVE: Shell of Wallace railroad depot.

TOP RIGHT: Burned forest, 1910.

All photos courtesy of the Library of Congress.

Photo by Clarence
E. Bisbee.

Twin Falls

Despite its current prominence in Southern Idaho, Twin Falls is one of the younger cities in the state. The earliest structure near the current city was the Rock Creek Stage Station south of town. In the 1860s, the station was one of the largest in Idaho and served stagecoach businessman Ben Holladay's traffic from Fort Hall to Boise. In 1865, James Bascom built the Rock Creek Store. Herman Stricker purchased the store in 1876 and operated it until 1897. That small settlement eventually grew into the town of Rock Creek.

Major development did not begin in the area until 1900 when I. B. Perrine created the Twin Falls Land and Water Company. His vision of bringing water out of the Snake River, down canals, and across the desert was a massive undertaking that nearly failed multiple times.

Perrine owned a ranch in the canyon near Blue Lakes and knew the potential of the dry lands on the north and south of the river's canyon walls. Along with Salt Lake businessman Stanley Milner, in 1905 Perrine was finally able to see his dream realized at Milner Dam.

Heavy advertising for the now-irrigated lands along with the financial benefits of the Carey Act — allowing private companies to erect irrigation systems and profit from the sales of water — resulted in a number of land drawings as each section of the valley opened to farming. On April 12, 1905, the city of Twin Falls was finally incorporated.

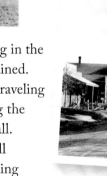

The new city grew rapidly as a center of commerce and farming in the Magic Valley. One of the primary drawbacks to the location remained. Getting from one rim of the canyon to the other required either traveling east and fording the river, or descending one canyon wall, crossing the river on a bridge or by ferry, and then scaling the other canyon wall. Perrine's ranch was in the middle of the shortest route, and his toll bridge brought him an additional source of income. The road leading down to Blue Lakes was chilling, but it was nothing compared to the hair-raising road that passed beneath Perrine Falls on the south wall of the canyon.

Eventually, advances in engineering prompted construction of soaring bridges. One near Perrine's ranch was named the Twin Falls – Jerome bridge (later renamed in honor of Perrine and then replaced with the current steel structure). The other bridge was built further east and south to serve the small town of Hansen. The original swinging Hansen toll bridge was later replaced with the current concrete structure.

Twin Falls also had the distinction of running the first electric storage battery railcars in the West. The short line ran from the city of Twin Falls to the magnificent Shoshone Falls. Unfortunately, that scheme did not work as well, but I. B. Perrine's legacy was already well established and the city he founded continued to grow.

OPPOSITE PAGE: Twin Falls, 1910.
Photo by Clarence E. Bisbee.

ABOVE: Land sale.

TOP RIGHT: Downtown Twin Falls, 1920s.

BOTTOM RIGHT: Rock Creek.

Nampa

Nampa's close relationship with the railroad ensured its growth. Among its citizens was Col. William H. Dewey, who made his fortune when he arrived in the Owyhee Mountains on foot and helped found Silver City. His fortune grew, and he eventually moved to Nampa where he pursued other business interests, among which was the Dewey Hotel. Opening on February 20, 1903 (a week before Dewey's death), his magnificent structure remained an important centerpiece of Nampa's life until it was torn down in 1963.

Like many other Idaho cities, Nampa's Main Street was a thriving center of the community. When the automobile arrived, car shows were a guaranteed event to draw a crowd to view the new offerings. The switch from horse-drawn vehicles to automobiles was so rapid that many Idahoans simply parked their buggies and put their horses out to pasture because nobody wanted to buy them!

TOP: Dewey Palace Hotel.

ABOVE: The fire rages through businesses.

Blasts from Nampa's past

At 3:00 p.m., July 3, 1909, a tramp walks into a cigar store at Twelfth and Front streets — a wood frame establishment with a large stock of fireworks for the big celebration. He picks up a firecracker and announces, "A bomb. I will set it off." The ignited fuse is tossed on the counter, setting off other fireworks. The resulting explosion blows out the front of the store and the fire quickly spreads to adjoining buildings. The city struggles to fight the inferno due to a water main being repaired and not enough hose to reach the fire. Business after business ignites and the bank becomes the center of the furnace.

The mayor makes calls to Boise and Caldwell for help. Caldwell's crew members loaded hose on an automobile and race to the aid of their brother firemen. Boise's chief Harry Fulton is absent, but his assistant Fred Lindsay springs into action, loading their steamer engine, a hose cart, and other equipment onto a special train. The Oregon Short Line locomotive makes the run in 18 minutes, an *average* of 60 miles per hour, the cruising speed of an express train! Undoubtedly, the column of smoke rising over the railroad city encouraged the engineer to let her fly.

Facing the fire

Nampa cannot wait for outside help. Business owners and their families try to pull belongings safely out of the fire's reach, but items sitting in the street continue to ignite from the intensity of the flames and falling embers. The owners scramble, trying to save what little they can. The beast threatens to swallow the city. Experienced men step forward and are allowed to dynamite wall after wall to slow the fire.

Just an hour after Mayor Dewey's frantic call, the Boise crew arrives. A water tender for a locomotive is stationed on a siding near the water tower to provide extra pressure for the fire engine. The Boise crew leans into the fight, but now firemen from Nampa, Boise, and Caldwell are stretched thin because they have to stop new blazes from escaping on neighboring blocks. The roof of the massive Dewey Hotel catches, but the luxury building is saved. At times, the heat is so intense the firemen are pushed back, but they persevere as concerned citizens watch and wonder what will happen.

Finally, after four agonizing hours, the conflagration is brought under control, but an entire city block in the heart of the business district is decimated. Nearby buildings show smoke and water damage. The Boise heroes do not return home until midnight. The damage is estimated to be at least $300,000, but insurance won't cover even half of that. Newspaper reports indicate the culprit who started the fire was never found. Storeowners claim the man was neither drunk nor crazy and not dressed like a tramp at all, telling *The Caldwell Tribune* that it was "just pure cussedness."

Down but not out

Nampa refuses to feel down, let alone out. One businessman is asked by a friend how he was faring in the wake of the devastation. His response is everything we would expect from an Idahoan. "Me? Oh, I'm all right. Burned out and broke; but there never was a better town than Nampa to be broke in, for there's always the big chance here. I'm going to remain, you bet, and start over again. Inside of six months I'll never know there had been a fire. I'll be housed in a better building and be doing a bigger business."

Every year on the fifth of July Nampa had put on a big show for people from all around the valley. Nampa promises that 1909 is going to be no different. *The Statesman* reports from Boise, "Those who lost their all in the fire will join as enthusiastically in the celebration tomorrow as though they had fat bank accounts. Nampa expects a large attendance. All who come will receive a royal welcome and the program is such the people of Nampa feel they will go away pleased." And so they did.

Rexburg

As Idaho entered the 20th century, small towns were the heart and soul of the state. With broad roads, small shops, local banks, theaters, and thriving religious communities, towns like Rexburg with their vibrant Main Streets united surrounding farming communities and provided important goods and services.

TOP: Rexburg.

RIGHT: Fremont Stake Tabernacle in Rexburg.

Sandpoint

The Mercantile was built in 1905 as was the Sandpoint Drug Company building next to it. The W. A. Berne building (with the awnings on the upper windows) was constructed in 1907. The Bigelow Hotel (with Cafe sign on the side) opened in 1909. Further down just beyond the horse wagon is the Northern Idaho News building (1915), one of the oldest frame-built structures in the historic district.

TOP: Sandpoint, after electricity, but before paved streets.

RIGHT: Like a number of other Idaho cities, Sandpoint operated a trolley streetcar system as an early form of mass transit.

The original bridge (circa 1910) crossing nearly two miles of Lake Pend Oreille from Sandpoint to Sagle was billed as the longest wooden bridge in the world. A lift was included that allowed for the passage of steamboats. The bridge had 1,540 pilings. It has been replaced thrice since 1910. Winters and WWII traffic took their toll on the wooden structure, and so the third and fourth were built with steel and concrete. The first two bridges were rotated slightly to the northwest of the current US-95 bridge. The original bridge ran straight to First Avenue in Sandpoint. From satellite views, the line of the old bridge can still be seen beneath the cold waters of Idaho's largest lake.

Salmon

Salmon is about 30 miles northwest of Lemhi Pass, where Lewis and Clark first entered what is now Idaho. The explorers famously met nearby with Sacagawea's brother, who helped by providing horses and directions through Idaho's formidable central wilderness.

Salmon grew as a settlement serving ranchers and miners near the Lemhi Shoshone reservation. As time progressed, it became a gateway into the wilderness area for hunters and adventurous rafters looking to float the famous "River of No Return" — the Salmon River.

TOP: Parade in Salmon, 1910s.

ABOVE: Bridge over Salmon River, c. 1905.

RIGHT: Steel bridge over Salmon River.

Moscow

Originally known as Hog Heaven and Paradise Valley, the town was first settled in 1871 and became known as Moscow after Samuel Neff filed for a postal permit in 1877. He said that the area reminded him of his home in Moscow, Pennsylvania. In May 1888, the U. S. Congress carved Latah County out of Nez Perce and named Moscow as the county seat. In 1889, the University of Idaho was created and placed in Moscow. The best evidence indicates that the events of 1888-1889 were compensations for the support of Moscow leaders against the decades-long movement to annex North Idaho into Washington.

TOP: Moscow Main Street, circa 1906.

LEFT: Federal Building, Moscow, circa 1911.
Photos courtesy of Manuscripts, Archives, and Special Collections, Washington State University Libraries.

LOGGING

ROSSI'S MILL, SHAFFER CREEK 20 MILES FROM BOISE CITY, BOISE CO. IDAHO.

Courtesy of Wallace W. Elliott & Co. "History of Idaho Territory," 1884.

When miners first arrived in Idaho, the two businesses that inevitably opened first were a lumber mill and a saloon. Idaho's vast forests provided abundant lumber for its rapidly growing cities, mines, and other businesses. At first, the mills were small affairs but the demand for harvested wood for constructing buildings, sluices, and cribbing quickly resulted in larger, world-famous operations, providing a good living for generations of loggers and lumbermen.

Fernwood

The Shay locomotive was a revolutionary invention ideal for logging. Power was sent to all wheels, resulting in better traction and pulling power on steep Idaho grades. U-joints and prismatic joints were used to accommodate the swiveling trucks. They could even run at partial slip rather than spinning the wheels and damaging the rails. The drive shaft is on the right side of the locomotive (and tender) as can be clearly seen in this historic photo.

Potlatch

Frederick Weyerhaeuser created the Potlatch Lumber Company in 1903. In 1904, the company assigned William Deary the job of locating a mill within the company's vast timber holdings. That same year, the company built the largest white pine sawmill in the world. Potlatch, Idaho, was born as a company town on the hills near the mill. In addition to 201 houses, Potlatch included boarding houses, an ice house, hotel, school, Catholic church, and a general store. Workers at the mill included scores of immigrants from Europe and even Japan.

The company even provided police, fire protection, a hospital, and recreational amenities for its workers. However, prostitution and alcohol were strictly prohibited within the town. Marriage was encouraged, since only married couples could rent company houses. Single men stayed in the boarding houses.

On September 11, 1906, the mill began operation and continued providing lumber for American homes until August of 1981 when it was finally closed due to declining lumber prices.

Where practicable, Idaho's abundant water resources were used to move logs off the mountains. Flumes like this one in Benewah, circa 1915, were man-made streams and rivers that could shunt logs from mountain gullies to rivers and other transportation points on the way to mills.

Following the Big Blowup fires of 1910, large stands of fire-killed white pine remained in the northern mountains of Idaho. Rather than leave the timber to rot, logging companies moved quickly to salvage as much of the wood as possible. Shay locomotives were pressed into heavy service with tracks often laid on bare ground without railroad ties, which were not needed for short-term use by the Shays. This photo shows the Milwaukee Lumber Company's sale area on Big Creek. While logging has been often blamed for the loss of Idaho's white pine forests, the loss of the state tree is due largely to the 1910 fire and devastation from European white pine blister rust. Idaho continues to rebuild white pine forests through better fire management and by breeding trees that are more resistant to blister rust. Still, it will be centuries before the forests approach their previous grandeur.

Spirit Lake Mill

Company towns dotted the Pacific Northwest, including Spirit Lake, Idaho, platted in 1907. The lumber mill processed logs from the forest east of Spokane and from Spirit Valley, producing 125,000 feet of lumber per 10-hour day. The millpond was described in the early 1900s as a "sea of logs" waiting to be moved through the mill.

Cutting timber is only the first step of the hard work required to make lumber. The logs must be moved from the forest to the sawmill. Initially, the work was done by sturdy draft horse breeds that could skid timber across the bare ground or using sleds on ice roads in the winter. Later, logging trucks and locomotives were used, but well into the 20th century, small operations and land owners skidded trees using horse power on ice roads.

Vowels Bros. logging truck, Wallace, circa 1921.

Photo courtesy of Barnard, T. N. (Thomas Nathan) photograph collections.

Barber

Few residents of the Treasure Valley realize that Barber was originally a lumber town with a large pond, dam, and lumber mill. The original plan was to float logs down the Boise River, but variable water levels made that impracticable except in a few scattered areas and at certain times of the year. Instead, cut logs were brought down via trains and were kept in the holding pond before they were transformed into lumber for Boise's growing needs. In the background, below the river bench, are multiple wagon tracks worn deeply into the soil. Those tracks were originally part of the Oregon Trail as it descended into the Boise area. By the time of this 1925 aerial photo, they were still being used by ranchers and others traveling to the valley from Soldier and Hill City, Idaho. Even today, the Oregon Trail ruts can be viewed above Barber to the east of Boise.

Photo by Captain A. W. Stevens, Army Air Corps, 1925.

Lewiston

For generations, Lewiston's operations were a critical part of America's lumber production. The position of the city at the confluence of the Snake and Clearwater rivers made it an ideal place to process logs into lumber. Similarly, the system of steamboats and later locks allowed Idaho to quickly ship finished lumber to the Pacific Ocean for easier transport. In August 1949, Idaho's first wood veneer plant opened at the site, followed in April 1951 by one of the world's largest pulp and paper mills. This 1938 photo shows the enormity of the operation at Lewiston.

Log drive

The flumes often ran to rivers where logs were held before they were guided downstream by "log drives" using the river current. Thousands of logs were floated by nimble-footed peavey crews, also known as river pigs, who moved logs out of slack water, ensured the logs did not jam, and cleared jams when they did occur. It was dangerous work!

The last major log drive in the United States occurred in 1971 on the Clearwater River. Logs floated 90 miles from the upper reaches of the North Fork down to the Potlatch mill at Lewiston. Log drives typically began in the spring with the runoff. The loggers brought with them a floating camp (called a wanigan) that consisted of a cookhouse and two bunkhouses tied together on rafts. Additional boats brought food, tools, and other equipment. The forest service recorded the 1971 drive, and the video footage can be viewed online. Once the Dworshak Dam was built near Orofino, the era of the log drives was over on the Clearwater.

TOP: River pigs.

RIGHT: Wanigan.

FAR RIGHT: Logs floating down the Clearwater River.

All photos courtesy of the US Forest Service.

EDUCATION

Boise Old Central School, New Central School

Many Boise residents know little to nothing of the first central school built to the west of the territorial capitol, where the Senate wing of the Idaho Capitol stands today. At the time, the citizens thought the school was too large, but they quickly found it was too small. A second Central School was built a block north on Washington Street, and the old building was used for a time for the state's deaf and blind. When the old building caught fire, it was demolished in anticipation of the new Capitol wing. Simultaneously, a new state school for the deaf and blind was planned first in Nampa but was eventually built in Gooding.

TOP: Old Central School.

Photo by M.M. Hazeltine.

LEFT: New Central School.

Boise High School, circa 1905

Badly designed, poorly constructed, and too small for the city's rapidly growing population, it was soon replaced with the newer, white brick building that stands today.

As noted by Steven Branting, Idaho's first incorporated town, Lewiston, levied the territory's first school tax in 1863. Its school district was the first to be chartered by the Territorial Legislature (1880), and the 1881 school board election featured two women candidates voted for by both men *and* women. In 1882, Lewiston became the site of the state's first institution of higher learning, Lewis Collegiate Institute (later Wilbur College). In 1914, the city opened the state's first junior high school and in 1965 became the first Idaho school district to adopt the team-teaching model.

The educational system of Idaho was pioneered, by many accounts, in Lewiston.

Lewiston State Normal School

Originally intended to be the site of Idaho's agricultural college because of the city's mild climate, Lewiston was a natural choice for the state's normal school. Created in January 1893, the college was essentially unfunded until 1895. The first class of 46 students began their classes in a local opera house in January 1896 as the 10-acre campus was being prepared on what would become known as Normal Hill.

Normal Schools originated in the 1500s when a group of schools in France became interested in improving teaching standards in a newly industrialized Europe. The term "normal" derived from the French école normale, a concept designed to establish educational norms and best practices. As settlers headed to the American West, there was a growing need for public education, and the Lewiston institution initially prepared teachers for the region's numerous one-room rural schools. Eventually, normal schools included vocational training so high school students could immediately enter the workforce after graduation.

In 1941, Glenn Todd, the college's new president, disliked the normal school moniker and ordered his own stationery which read North Idaho Teachers College. He also preferred to be called the president of the school rather than principal. His stationery apparently delivered, and people soon adopted the contemporary name.

Photo by Bruce Burns, 1926.

It was not all about vanity though. Education was changing and the normal school model was being replaced by the teachers college model in much of the country. Teachers colleges granted bachelor's degrees that were quickly becoming a requirement for certification.

Politicians and the state board of education became concerned that Todd was exceeding his authority with the name change. Yet they also realized that the normal school model was on its way out. In 1943, the state Board of Education made the school into a four-year college. Although the name North Idaho Teachers College found its way into newspapers and onto postcards, it was never official.

Leadership at the school balked at the new name and informally christened the institution the Northern Idaho College of Education. The Legislature resisted for a while, but in 1947 the school was officially renamed Northern Idaho College of Education, which was nice (and had the acronym NICE which was also nice).

That name was short-lived. In 1951, the state legislature decided it was spending entirely too much money on education, and both NICE and the SICE (at Albion in southern Idaho) were closed in favor of other colleges in the state assuming all teacher education. The decision was a disaster since the growing state population inevitably included more children and children required teachers. While the state's colleges enjoyed getting the additional funding, they failed to properly predict the increasing demand for instructors and couldn't train and accredit educators quickly enough to fill positions. Idaho was left in the embarrassing position of having to grant a large number of provisional teaching certificates to assuage the teaching shortage.

Eventually recognizing the severity of the error, the legislature changed its position in 1955 and reopened the Lewiston school as the Lewis–Clark Normal School. As well as referencing the original, dated title, it was still a two-year school and was subordinate to the University of Idaho in Moscow. That arrangement fell apart in 1963 as accreditation problems came to a head.

The state elevated the school to a four-year institution in 1963, but it wasn't funded until 1965. The upgrade offered students an opportunity to earn bachelor's degrees and the college to expand its curriculum to include vocational education and nursing, both in high demand. In 1971, the school name was officially changed to Lewis–Clark State College. It was the last institution in the country to stop using the term "Normal School" as part of its name.

Albion State Normal School

Like Lewiston's Normal school, the Albion school was built in Cassia County to train teachers in southern Idaho. As was the case at Lewiston State Normal, female students were required to be a minimum of 15 years of age, and boys had to be at least 16 years old to enroll. Students attended for one to three years to be able to teach, and four years to earn a permanent teaching certificate. The Albion school closed in 1951 after having trained approximately 6,000 teachers. Following the school's closing, teachers were trained in Pocatello.

Pocatello High School

Pocatello's first school was a multi-use building owned by the railroad, shown here in 1885. Once the town became established, in 1892 the citizens quickly began to build a new stone school on the west side of town. Amazingly, the original walls still exist in the current Pocatello High School beneath a newer facade.

In 1895, another school was built on the east side of the railroad tracks, and the west side school soon became the high school.

In 1901 and 1903, wings were added to the school to accommodate the city's rapidly growing student population.

The school suffered a major setback when a large fire broke out on December 16, 1914. The center and northern wings were badly damaged, but the walls and the southern wing remained.

Noted architect Frank Paradice was hired to redesign the school's remaining south wing and fill the burned shell of the north wing and central sections. The reconstructed school opened in 1916.

Once again, overcrowding became a problem, and in 1939 the school was renovated for a second time under the guiding hand of Frank Paradice, as part of the Works Progress Administration program. The wings of the building were expanded, and a new facade was designed to cover the old walls. The building was further expanded in 1968 and 2005. The most recent addition was just completed in December of 2021.

LEFT: 1885.

BELOW: 1903.

BOTTOM LEFT: Fire in 1914.

BOTTOM RIGHT: 1917.

University of Idaho – Southern Branch

In 1901, Idaho Governor Frank W. Hunt signed a bill that established the Academy of Idaho in Pocatello. Classes began in 1902 and by 1910 there were approximately 300 students enrolled. In 1915, the school was renamed Idaho Technical Institute.

In 1927, it was renamed as University of Idaho – Southern Branch and continued to operate as a two-year school, shown here in a 1932 photograph.

In 1947, the school was made into a four-year college and renamed Idaho State College. Finally, in 1963, it was renamed to Idaho State University.

Photo courtesy of the US Army Air Corps.

LEFT: Old Administration Building.

BELOW LEFT: New Administration Building.

University of Idaho at Moscow

On January 30, 1889, Idaho Territorial Governor Edward Stevenson signed legislation establishing the University of Idaho at Moscow as the new state's land-grant institution. The university opened nearly four years later on October 3, 1892. The placement in Moscow was an important concession to quiet political agitation in the territory's panhandle region by residents who wanted to join Washington rather than be part of Idaho.

In 1906, the original Administration Building burned. When the building did not fully collapse, the school of mines at U of I dynamited the rock walls. A new Tudor Gothic administration building was constructed in 1909.

ABOVE: 1932.

LEFT: BSU Admin
Building.
Photo courtesy of Wikimedia
Commons, photographer:
Iamneven.

Boise State University

What is now Boise State University had its humble beginnings in 1932 as Boise Junior College, a religious institution operated by the Episcopal Church at St. Margaret's Hall. In 1934 the church ended its affiliation with the school when a board of directors assumed leadership.

The school was moved in 1940 to the site of the old Boise Airport. At that time a new administration building opened (shown) and a football stadium was built at the current site of the Student Union Building.

In 1965, the school began offering baccalaureate degrees, and enrollment reached 5,000. Accordingly, it was renamed Boise College. Just four years later, the school was renamed Boise State College. Its final name was set in 1974 when the school was granted university status, and it became Boise State University.

CAPITOL

Goose Creek House

Built in 1862 on the Packer John Trail leading from Lewiston to Boise City, Goose Creek House (right) was the site of the first Democratic Party Convention in the new Idaho Territory in October 1863.

Idaho's first territorial governor, William Wallace, chose Lewiston to be the capital, primarily because of its access to the West Coast. Wallace rented a livery store for his office, along with the city school, its Masonic Lodge, and a few storefronts to serve as legislative chambers and committee meeting rooms.

Left: The governor's office.

Boise Territorial Capitol

The second territorial and first state capitol of Idaho.

State Capitol

The first state capitol was built on State Street in Boise in the mid-1880s when Idaho was still a territory. Construction began on the current capitol in 1905 and finished in 1920. As seen below in a 1912 photograph, the new capitol is under construction, with the old capitol on the right and Central School on the left. Both the school and the first capitol were razed after the completion of the central section of the new capitol. The additional space was then used for the new building's wings.

GREAT DEPRESSION

Sandy soil blown against fence, Oneida County.

Photo by Arthur Rothstein, 1915-1985, May 1936.

Part of a family of 14 lived in this chuck wagon in Oneida County.

Photo by Arthur Rothstein, 1915–1985, May 1936.

A large family on land too poor to give them a living, Oneida County.

Photo by Arthur Rothstein, 1915-1985, May 1936.

Son of sheep rancher, Oneida County.

Photo by Arthur Rothstein, 1915-1985, May 1936.

A submarginal farm purchased by Resettlement Administration to be returned to grazing land, Oneida County.

Photo by Arthur Rothstein, 1915-1985, May 1936.

Abandoned church in cut-over area, Boundary County.

Photo by Dorothea Lange, October 1939.

A farmer prepares to remove a tamarack stump, Bonner County. It would take 14 sticks of dynamite.

Photo by Dorothea Lange, October 1939.

This sawmill carriage and log turner were made by these farmers at the Ola self-help sawmill co-op. Gem County.

Photo by Dorothea Lange, October 1939.

Tamarack, Adams County

This town is nearly deserted since the sawmill shut down.

Photo by Dorothea Lange, October 1939.

WORLD WAR II

Farragut Naval Training Station, Idaho Class 218, circa 1943. *Photo courtesy of the US Navy.*

Farragut

Farragut was a US Navy training school at the south end of Lake Pend Oreille at Bayview. Named after Admiral David Farragut, the training center provided 293,000 sailors with basic training over 30 months. The last recruit graduated in March 1945.

Pocatello Army Air Base

In 1942, the US Army announced it would spend $3 million dollars to build a training base west of Pocatello. The goal was to train B-17 and B-24 bomber pilots and crews as well as support aircraft pilots flying P-47 Thunderbolts. It is believed that one of the reasons the location was chosen was the belief that if pilots could handle the strong, constant winds of Pocatello then they could fly anywhere.

While that may be apocryphal, the location was especially attractive for other reasons. Pocatello's railroad hub facilitated movement of troops and the Arco desert with lava "islands" made an excellent bombing range for the trainees.

The young pilots had mishaps, and 16 people lost their lives in crashes before the base was decommissioned.

ABOVE: Trainees in front of a P-47 Thunderbolt.

TOP RIGHT: Pilots at Pocatello Army Air Base.

BOTTOM RIGHT: Main gate of air base.

All photos courtesy of the US Army.

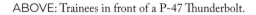

Naval Ordinance Plant

In April 1942, the United States Navy opened a gun plant just north of Pocatello (today the grounds are inside the city limits). The massive facility was designed to refurbish 16-inch cannon barrels for the Navy's battleships. Primarily, the work done was relining the barrels and then sending them to an installation near Arco for testing. Pocatello's railroad hub and location inland made it an ideal location for the work. After the war, the plant was decommissioned, but that testing site in the desert was to become the national nuclear laboratory.

TOP: Naval gun plant from the air.

RIGHT: Battleship gun being refurbished.

All photos courtesy of the US Department of Defense.

LEFT: Cookies for the All Idaho Marine Platoon traveling through Pocatello.

BELOW: Boise Depot with canteen.

USO Huts

Patriotism ran high in Idaho during WWII, and the endless flow of soldiers and sailors along the railroad lines brought out the best in many Idahoans. In Boise, a "canteen" was opened at the Union Pacific depot to provide the servicemen and women with coffee and a bite to eat.

In Pocatello, a group of women were committed to ensuring every person serving in the military got something to drink and a cookie. Their organizational skills even garnered national media attention in the June 1944 *National Geographic*. Cookie drives were conducted in every city within driving distance. A USO hut opened by the railroad, and the women served cookies and hot or cold drinks to trainloads of service members night and day.

Other communities similarly stepped up to make service members feel welcome. The whole nation was pulling together for the war effort, and Idaho was determined not to be left out.

NUCLEAR AGE

National Nuclear Reactor Testing Station

Admiral Hyman G. Rickover (right) was the driving force behind the nuclear program at the reactor testing station. His dream of nearly silent submarines with unlimited range became a reality. At the same time, he pioneered nuclear safety and engineering principles that are still used today.

In the late 1940s and early 1950s, the United States greatly increased research into nuclear science. The reactor testing station in the Eastern Idaho desert became one of the most important sites for that research. Established at the naval gun test range on the Big Lost River, the desert experiment station became a hive of activity. Former war-era residential housing (seen here near the water tower) was quickly deemed insufficient, and additional civilian housing was built around an oval with two larger apartment buildings nearby. Today, "the site" is officially known as the Idaho National Laboratory near Arco, but it looks very different from this photo. Nearly every structure in this picture has been removed or extensively remodelled. Two of the original residential buildings still stand, as does the barracks for the Marines who guarded the guns, explosives and projectiles used to test the mighty battleship guns of WWII after they were re-lined at Pocatello.

Photos courtesy of the US Department of Energy.

Sub testing

Shown here is the test hull designed to simulate the interior of a submarine. Inside this hull, the first fully functional naval nuclear power plant was tested. Future testing included placing a mock-up of a submarine in a large pool and rocking it side to side while the reactor was operating. Placed at intervals around the pool, underwater microphones were ready to catch any sound that escaped the sub walls. Admiral Rickover's order was to make the submarines as silent as possible and his team did just that. Today, there is a conning tower from a submarine parked in the Arco desert near the location where the world's first nuclear submarine was designed and tested. It took just over two years (August 1950 until January 1954) before the nuclear powered Nautilus (SSN-571) launched.

Photo courtesy of the US Department of Energy.

Reactor testing

The Idaho National Laboratory was at the forefront of the nuclear power generation. For about an hour on July 17, 1955, Arco, Idaho was the first community in the United States (or the world) to have its lights powered solely by nuclear energy.

Power was supplied by Argonne National Laboratory's BORAX-III reactor (a boiling water nuclear reactor) at the nearby National Reactor Testing Station (NRTS). BORAX-III provided 2,000 kilowatts to power Arco and the BORAX test facility, and partially powered the National Reactor Testing Station. Shown here are different views of the BORAX-III reactor and the control room.

Photo courtesy of the US Department of Energy.

Photos courtesy of the US Department of Energy.

Reactor accident

As seen in an exterior view on the top right, the Argonne Lower Power Reactor (ALPR) facility designed for the United States Army with the hopes that similar reactors could be used for remote radar outposts in places like the Arctic. In 1958, the Army took over the facility to train soldiers to operate the reactor, which was powered by uranium-enriched fuel plates. These plates sustained a nuclear chain reaction, which heated water into steam to generate electricity. The reaction could be controlled by raising or lowering the reactor's five control rods.

Unfortunately, the reactor had a design flaw. An operator could fully remove a control rod, resulting in a runaway nuclear chain reaction, called a meltdown.

On December 23, 1960, the reactor was shut down for maintenance with a restart scheduled for the first week of January. On the evening of January 3, 1961, three soldiers were working on the reactor when one man raised the rod much higher than needed. In under four milliseconds the core melted and exploded. The force of the pressure wave drove superheated steam upward, where it collided with the top of the pressure vessel at 159 feet per second. The vessel failed to contain the pressure, and radioactive water and debris exploded into the room.

The accident killed two men instantly. The third died about two hours later. While there have long been rumors that the event might have been a murder-suicide related to an extramarital affair, there is no proof of those accusations, and the accident was attributed to poor reactor design and insufficient training.

It was the world's first reactor accident, and emergency crews were largely unprepared to handle the situation. While scientists checked radiation on Highway 20, a radioactive cloud was detected moving south from the site before eventually dissipating. General Electric was assigned the task of removing the reactor vessel, along with safely dismantling and disposing of the contaminated buildings. Work on the cleanup was conducted in 1961 and 1962.

The events at SL-1 are now part of the required safety training in nuclear programs around the world. Soon a photograph of the melted reactor (seen at right) was placed on a safety poster and displayed where engineers would be reminded of the dangers faced when working with nuclear power.

Photos courtesy of the US Department of Energy.

Idaho National Laboratory

Today, the Idaho National Laboratory continues its work into nuclear research, as well as investigations into drones, communications, and numerous other technical experiments. The scientists and engineers work with space-age technology just yards from the Goodale North Alternate portion of the Oregon Trail. Near their desert laboratories lie stagecoach roads, and across the site there is an old, failed irrigation system that was intended to facilitate farming in the region before WWII. To the west of the site is Craters of the Moon National Monument. To its the north are the rugged mountains that channel the Big Lost and Little Lost Rivers down into the valley

Idaho continues to live in the past, present, and future as we preserve our history, live our lives, and help shape the future of not only Idaho, but also the world.

ABOVE: Advanced test reactor.
Photo courtesy of the US Department of Energy.

LEFT: Atomic City gas station.
Photo by Justin Smith.

Kendrick

You might be forgiven for thinking Kendrick in North Central Idaho is no place special. The community in Latah County boasts only about 350 people, but its sleepy streets don't begin to tell the whole story of this tiny village in a narrow canyon.

Originally called Latah after the county's name, the town remained relatively unchanged until around 1890 when the road for the iron horse was announced. The quick-thinking postmaster, Thomas Kirby, brokered a deal with Northern Pacific to convince the company to extend track to the town by January 1, 1891. In return, Mr. Kirby would deed half the town (120 acres) to the railway giant. To seal the deal, the community was renamed Kendrick after Northern Pacific's chief engineer.

On May 8, 1890, Kendrick was duly platted, and by mid-October it was incorporated. Although the first locomotive did not pull in until February 4, 1891, the slight delay was more than made up for as the company set up a yard for servicing its trains on the free chunk of land.

The newly renamed town soon became a hub to serve a growing population of 600 citizens, as well as folk from surrounding small communities. Shops and businesses catered to patrons in need of banking services, building materials, groceries, medicines, mining supplies, and luxury items. Four livery stables served the freight needs of the locals, while two doctors and two churches tended to their bodies and souls. The school was at capacity, and the elegant St. Elmo Hotel became a popular destination for lodging.

Conflagration

On August 16, 1892, one and a half years after the railroad brought prosperity to the region, a flame at the newspaper office turned into a conflagration that decimated 31 businesses resulting in losses of $100,000. The only non-residential structure left standing was the

Kendrick's streets flooded January 12, 1900. *Photo courtesy of Steven R. Shook.*

little train depot. As often happened in the West, the town rebuilt quickly, with most structures constructed from wood.

Kendrick's troubles were far from over. On December 15, 1899, a double-header train with 19 cars loaded with steel rails went out of control traveling on the long downgrade from Troy. Both locomotives lost traction as they attempted to descend the hill during a light afternoon snow flurry.

The train screamed down the six miles of track, derailed near Kendrick, tipped, and then broke apart. A large portion of the wreck ended in the river. Both engineers and a fireman died at the scene. The best the newspapers could do was to say the men were "horribly mutilated." The other fireman and a brakeman died days later from their injuries.

The two men in the caboose decided that living with desertion and unemployment was better than dying with valor and unemployment. They uncoupled before it was too late and came to a safe stop. Even if their decision was understandable, no railroader would ever trust them with their lives again, and they were fired.

The tracks were destroyed for a quarter mile. The massive cargo was wrenched apart, and steel rails were launched into mangled heaps 250 feet from the damaged track. Flatcars had flown through the air and tumbled along the ground; at least one came to rest 100 feet from the right of way.

The cataclysm was not yet done though. The wreck partially dammed the Potlatch River. It was December so the railroad let the immobile rails sit on the frozen river while they repaired the tracks.

Less than a month after the accident, a strong Chinook wind sent three days of rain, melted the snow pack and sent water and driftwood racing down the river. As the steel rails caught the driftwood the dam grew larger even as the waters rose. The stream's current lashed at the railroad embankment that fell away, allowing the water to edge into town as the daylight dwindled.

An angry river

The Potlatch released her fury. Within minutes the water grew from a trickle to a roaring river several feet deep in the middle of town. Buildings simply floated away.

A newspaper put it succinctly. "The Potlatch River is a raging torrent and the worst flood in its history is resulting in great damage to property. The lower part of Kendrick is under water and in some of the residences... six feet of water covers the floors. Eight miles of railroad track are washed out between this point and Vollmer, and below here a bridge and considerable track are gone. At the railroad yards there is a foot of water and the track is being washed out there. The water is now creeping into the stores on the lower side of the street and is rising at the rate of eight inches an hour."

Residents evacuated to the nearby bluffs, wading or swimming through the icy waters to save their lives. A family in a buggy trying to escape the flood was besieged by 40 cords of wood lifted and carried by the enraged river. The horses panicked. A wheel struck a curb, and the buggy tipped. Mr. and Mrs. Charles Hamlin's three little girls fell into the torrent. Mr. Hamlin was saved, pulled from the waters by a man named John Long. A second couple in the buggy barely survived by holding onto each other with their child between them, but Mrs. Hamlin and her three daughters could not be found.

Many others narrowly missed a watery grave. A hero on horseback saved 15 of his neighbors from a single building. Over 30 buildings were destroyed or damaged beyond repair. Four homes were lost entirely.

In the morning's light, an agonized wail was heard over Kendrick's flooded streets. Mrs. Hamlin was found in the top floor of a building clinging to life "half dead from exposure and anguish." Her three little girls were still missing.

Facing the challenge

Once again, the citizens of Kendrick cleared the debris, rebuilt, and set about life, presumably unaware that more troubles were to come. On August 4, 1904, another major fire swept through town. This time 43 businesses and 19 homes went up in smoke. In three hours the entire business portion of the town was in ashes.

Kendrick responded with fierce determination. Tempered like fine steel annealed, forged, hardened, and quenched, the people sprung back to life with practiced ease, opening tents and shacks as shops, churches, and schoolrooms. The council passed a new regulation mirroring those in other parts of Idaho: commercial buildings must be constructed with bricks. Within a year, 20 fine brick buildings stood on Kendrick's streets.

Such heartache and resolve built Idaho. Beneath the modern cities are foundations of blood, sweat, determination, and many tears. Still, it is a beautiful land of soaring peaks, sweeping vistas, singing bluebirds, and delicate syringa. It's our home.